363.34/81/0971Mel

Heartbreak and Heroism

Also by John Melady

Explosion

Escape from Canada!

Korea: Canada's Forgotten War

Cross of Valour

The Little Princes

Overtime, Overdue: The Bill Barilko Story

Pilots

Heartbreak and Heroism
Canadian Search and Rescue Stories

John Melady

Dundurn Press
Toronto • Oxford

Editor: Derek Weiler
Designer: Scott Reid
Printer: Transcontinental Printing Inc.

Canadian Cataloguing in Publication Data

Melady, John
     Heartbreak and heroism

ISBN 1-55002-287-3

1. Canada.   Canadian Armed Forces — Search and rescue operations — History.   I. Title

UG635.C2M44 1997   363.34'81'0971   C97-931749-5

1 2 3 4 5 SR 01 00 99 98 97

We acknowledge the support of the **Canada Council for the Arts** for our publishing program. We also acknowledge the support of the **Ontario Arts Council** and the **Book Publishing Industry Development Program** of the **Department of Canadian Heritage**.

Printed and bound in Canada.

Printed on recycled paper.

Dundurn Press
8 Market Street
Suite 200
Toronto, Ontario, Canada
M5E 1M6

Dundurn Press
73 Lime Walk
Headington, Oxford
England
OX3 7AD

Dundurn Press
250 Sonwil Drive
Buffalo, NY
U.S.A. 14225

Contents

To Mary and Glenn Butters —
for your encouragement and assistance
in Edmonton and elsewhere.

Acknowledgements

I wanted to write this book for some time, but other topics seemed to present themselves in more pressing ways. Finally however, after much encouragement and gentle nudging from my friends Barb and K.O. Simonson, I began to research these stories. This little volume is the result. It is not, nor was it intended to be, a definitive history of Search and Rescue in Canada. It is simply a selective snapshot of Para Rescue personnel and the good work they do.

As with any book, several people deserve to be thanked for their advice, assistance and direction in making the project a reality. Because I was an outsider looking at a unique and rather closed field of endeavour, I had to ask some very fundamental questions to understand what Search and Rescue was all about. Several people went out of their way to be helpful, and patiently responded to my most naive entreaties. I thank them. In addition to those whose names appear in the text, I also want to express my gratitude to the following: Steve Andrews, Gary Arsenault, Bill and Lana Barnicke, Wally Bastarache, Jeff Brace,

Ken Clark, Bernie and Teresa Cline, Rob Colthard, Louise Crone, Debra Drysdale, John Edwards, Ralph Gorcey, Earl Hewison, Tom Iannella, Len Jackson, Ben Lafrance, Ron MacDonald, Wally Marshall, Stevo McNeil, Wayne McCrae, Bruce Nickson, Tom Nigro, Carol O'Rourke–Elliott, Vince Otterson, Rob Quinn, Jayanti Roy, Danno Schut, Steve Snider, Ian Stock, Terry Swanson, Bob Teather, Pat Tighe, Gerry Wile, and Joe and Marilyn Williams.

All writers owe certain people for whatever success a book may have. In my case, several individuals deserve a special mention. Foremost among them is my wife Mary, who has heard me tell all these stories but still puts up with me. Others include Esther Parry, whose close-to-deadline keyboarding skills continue to amaze me; Major Joan Gordon and Captain Dan Chicoyne, who were so helpful during my time at RCC Trenton; Mike Johnston, for his patience, good humour, and assistance in helping me locate several of the people whose stories are in this book; Cliff Fielding, for his wit, wisdom, and unique perspective on things military; Colonel Brad Gibbons, for letting me hang out with, fly with, and talk to anyone I needed; Captains Eric Esdale and Mike Janke for their assistance and direction; my editor, Derek Weiler, for his fine work on the manuscript; Scott Reid, for his wonderful design work, and especially Kirk Howard, for his enthusiasm for this project and his decision to publish it. My thanks to all.

John Melady,
Brighton, Ontario
July, 1997

A SAR Tech prepares to land by parachute. (Canadian Forces photo)

The cockpit of a Labrador helicopter. (Canadian Forces photo)

Two SAR Techs are hoisted into a Labrador helicopter. (Canadian Forces photo)

Labrador helicopter flight engineer Wally Marshall at a spotter's window during a training flight.

SAR Tech Steve Andrews at a spotter's window of a Hercules aircraft. The window may be removed when a search is not in progress.

SAR Tech Pat Tighe is shown as he is hoisted into a Labrador helicopter during a training flight. Several of the people mentioned in this book were lifted from danger in a similar fashion.

The crowded interior of a Labrador helicopter during a training flight.

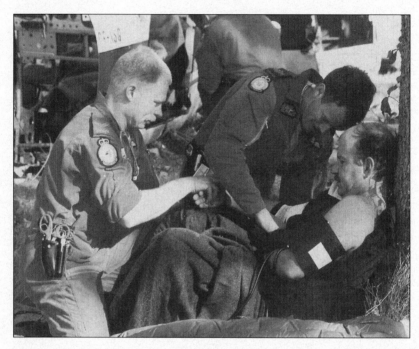

SAR Techs work on a "casualty" following a simulated training crash. Personnel in Canada's Search and Rescue operations must be prepared to face almost any medical emergency. (Canadian Forces photo)

A group of current and former SAR Techs gathers for the Para Rescue cairn dedication at the RCAF Memorial Museum in Trenton, Ontario on May 31, 1997.

Introduction

"That Others May Live" is the motto of the Para Rescue Association of Canada. It is a simple concept, straightforward, evocative, yet rich with meaning and worth. It is low-key, self-effacing, timeless. And to the members of the Association, the meaning of the motto is their reason for being.

Established by federal government mandate in 1947, Search and Rescue has now been an official organization in Canada for fifty years, although its origins go back a bit earlier. But in all that time, the men and women who pursued its purposes were always there to help, to perform their duties in the services of others. What they did, and continue to do, is the subject matter of this book.

The volume is not, nor was it intended to be, a definitive history of Search and Rescue in Canada. It is merely a compilation of Search and Rescue stories told, in most cases, by those who lived them. The emphasis, as will be seen, is on the Air Force involvement in the field — the involvement of those brave souls who were or are Para Rescue people. There are also many others who seek and save in Canada, but these stories are not theirs, although their efforts are no less commendable.

For the most part, those involved in Para Rescue are a relatively close-knit group of individuals. They face the same obstacles, share similar triumphs, and suffer alike when things go wrong. Virtually all are competitive, determined, enterprising and inventive. Many are risk-takers; most are self-starters. All are dedicated in ways seldom seen in other professions. These are their stories.

1

The Birth of Para Rescue

It is generally acknowledged that W.R. "Wop" May was the father of Search and Rescue in Canada. The legendary bush pilot, who won the Distinguished Flying Cross in World War I following his encounters with the Red Baron and other German fliers, found himself again assisting the Allied cause in World War II. This time around, he was the civilian manager of what was called 2 Air Observer School in Edmonton, Alberta. The school helped to train young men for overseas duty as navigators and air observers.

In the course of his duties in this role, May became acutely aware of the number of young pilots who, while flying in the north, had engine trouble, became lost, disoriented, or otherwise incapacitated and ended up crashing into the trackless tundra or bush, often far from civilization. And even if they survived the crash itself, pilots were often doomed to die from starvation or a host of other causes. In the winter, they had to deal with the cold as well, and many froze to death and were never found.

May determined to do what he could to put an end to this state of affairs. After much discussion, investigation, and personal lobbying, he decided to form his own Search and Rescue (SAR) organization. Its members would be highly trained, physically fit, and capable of parachuting to air crashes to render medical aid. In May's view, if such a team could save lives, it would serve its purpose.

He looked south, to the American state of Montana, for his inspiration. There, at the small city of Missoula, near the confluence of Clark Fork and the Bitterroot River, the United States Forestry Service ran a school where parachuting was part of the curriculum. The students learned parachute jumping, not for life saving but for fighting forest fires. They flew to where fires were, then jumped to fight them.

May decided to adopt their methods for his purposes.

"The fact that Wop decided to check out the Montana Smoke Jumpers was a stroke of genius," his old friend and fellow bush pilot Punch Dickins told this author years later. "They had been parachuting into the bush for years, and they were damned good at it. Wop learned from them, and then he sent some of his boys down there for training. He even borrowed some equipment, I believe."

Dickins was correct. Parachute clothing, particularly for jumps into the bush, was not yet available in Canada. Most of the material used was canvas, with extra padding here and there, and a higher than usual waistband. The collar was also high, in order to afford jumpers as much protection as possible when they came down into trees. A modified leather football helmet and a wire mesh face mask completed the outfit. It was a far cry from the lightweight, space-age clothing used by jumpers today, but for the time it was practical, functional, and in due course, readily available.

The first Canadian jumpers were trained at Missoula, but within weeks were back in Canada, perfecting their skills and instructing others in the techniques learned. Some months afterwards, May's men were absorbed into the Royal Canadian

Air Force (RCAF), and Para Rescue was henceforth a part of the military. It still is.

Three months before the German surrender in Europe, the first of two wartime Para Rescue courses began in Edmonton. Classroom instruction was done there, while actual parachuting and bush lore were taught at Jasper, Alberta. The first commanding officer was Flight Lieutenant Stan Knapp while the medical officer was Flight Lieutenant Nicholas Woywitka, M.D. Twelve men passed the fifteen-week course — which was tough, interesting, and ever-evolving. It included rudimentary medical training (some of which was done in hospitals), parachute jumping, signalling, supply-dropping, bush survival, mountain climbing, and hours and hours of physical fitness. Those who graduated felt they were in the best shape of their lives.

The medical instruction dealt with everything from treatment of shock, burns, snowblindness, and haemorrhage to the proper application of splints, methods of artificial respiration and the transport of injured persons. Medical kits for para-drops were developed by the Air Rescue School and included, in the terminology of the time, "House Wife Kits," which were sewing materials for patching torn clothing and darning woolen socks. And because cigarettes were then regarded as vital in any Arctic rations, they were packed as well.

When it came to parachuting, students trained first by jumping from a high wooden platform, generally known as "the Tower." They were dressed in jump gear and were severely jolted when the rope tied to the top of the structure became taut. The jolt was meant to simulate the shock of a parachute opening. No one loved the tower, nor were they enamoured with some of the other training methods used — one of which was to jump off the back of a moving truck, and then do a roll. One student complained of a sore shoulder: as he rolled, his shoulder hit a pile of frozen elk manure.

The actual jumping from planes was the highlight of the course for most participants. It was exciting, dangerous, and — particularly the first time — unforgettable. While the number of jumps was left up to the instructor/jumpmaster, generally at least ten were done — four of which were into the bush. A minimum of eight jumps were required for graduation.

Finally, however, each course ended, and graduates were posted to locations where their newly acquired talents could best be used. By the time the second course finished, Word War II was over — yet the need for qualified Para Rescue people did not end.

In 1947, the first peacetime course was held.

Clifford W. "Bounce" Weir was named the commanding officer. An outgoing, bombastic RCAF veteran, Weir was an excellent choice for the position. He was authoritative, direct, generally well liked, and good at the job. A native of Dauphin, Manitoba and a pilot, he had known Wop May for years, and was as keen as his mentor to make the school both successful and respected. He remained as commanding officer for several courses. As well, some of his students came back as instructors; two of these, Steve Trent and Ken Clark, have remained keenly interested in the courses ever since.

Some years ago, when Para Rescue included nursing sisters, four young women posed for this photograph. All are wearing jump uniforms. They are (L to R): Marion Neily, Isabel Thomson, Marion McDonald, and Ann Pedden. (Photo courtesy of Bill Krier)

In the early years, non-medical aspirants made up most of the student body. By 1951, however, more and more young people with medical backgrounds were accepted. They were doctors, hospital assistants, and in that year and the next, nursing sisters — all of whom were expected to complete the same rigorous training as the men. This included bush work, mountain climbing and parachute jumping.

It is said that Bounce Weir took a little more time than others to get used to the new environment. Much later, he used to tell a story illustrating his gradual understanding of just what women could do, and how they were just as competent in Para Rescue as men. One day, after Weir had watched a group of nursing sisters demonstrate the setting up of a bush camp, he was somewhat vocal in criticizing one of them. The woman, whom he did not name, but who was physically quite small and fine-featured, took him aside after the evening meal. She then asked him to accompany her to a grove of small trees nearby. Weir noticed that she had an axe in her hand.

When they got to the grove, the student drew Weir's attention to one little tree with a trunk that separated and made a "Y" a few feet from the ground. The young woman then moved to a second tree and instructed Weir to watch. She cut down the second tree with half a dozen swings of the axe. When the chopped tree fell, its trunk came down with a thud, right in the centre of the Y of the first tree.

The woman then turned to Bounce Weir and said, "When *you* can do that, you can tell me off. Until then, keep your criticism to yourself." Weir got the point, and always enjoyed recalling how it was made.

In the first few years of Canadian Para Rescue, the parachutes used were something less than technical marvels. "We had very poor equipment at the outset," recalls L.J. "Dutch" Franks. "And you couldn't do much with it, unless you made a lot of modifications. We experimented, tried different things. Some worked. Some did not. That included parachutes and just about everything else. When I started, the parachutes were thirty-two-foot, flat, circular things called the Derry Slot. They came in around 1942, but they were used until 1966 or so. We modified them using soldering irons so the nylon would melt. What we did made them illegal, I suppose, but they were no good the way they were originally. It took fifteen seconds to do a half-turn in the air. There were no brakes, and you had almost no way of controlling your drift.

"One way of getting down fast was to go out low — at eight hundred feet instead of the twelve hundred we were supposed to go out at. Because the longer you were in the air, the farther you drifted. It was a very poor chute. And even if it got you down okay, you generally had a long walk because you had probably drifted far from the target. Then when they opened, the Derry Slots tore your head off. You were supposed to keep your head down. But when you have just jumped from the plane and you are at eight hundred feet, and the chute has not opened, it's hard to resist looking up to see if the rigging is tangled.

A Royal Canadian Air Force Para Rescue Specialist demonstrates the difficulty of parachuting from the blister window of the Canso aircraft. (RCAF photo)

Invariably, as soon as you raised your head, the damned thing would open with a loud *bang*! and you would see lots of stars — in the middle of the day.

"We jumped from different kinds of planes of course, but to my mind, parachuting from the old Canso was something else. There was no ramp, or even a proper door to leave from. You went out through this little blister on the side of the plane. There was a little seat at the opening of the blister. The seat had four legs, two long legs at the front and two short ones at the back. You sat on this thing, then half climbed over the edge of the blister, held onto the leading edge, and got ready. Then when it was time to go, the jumpmaster would whack you on the back, and you would fall out of the plane. You couldn't stand up or anything; you just flopped off the edge."

By all accounts, the camaraderie on the Para Rescue courses was always good. This included the two years in which women

Grace Woodman at Sea Island, British Columbia the night before she parachuted to the slopes of a mountain where a man had punctured his lung in a fall. Today, as Grace MacEachern, she holds the same helmet she wore as a Para Rescue Nursing Sister.

accompanied the men. One of those women was Grace MacEachern, a nurse, whose name was Grace Woodman when she was accepted for, then successfully completed, Course #6 in 1952. "We all got along well," she recalls. "The men could do some things better than the women, but we could do things the men had trouble doing. We helped each other. I have fond memories of Para Rescue School."

Almost always, fresh graduates found themselves on searches for lost planes, lost people, and in a host of other situations in which Para Rescue personnel were required. In her case, Grace Woodman did not have long to wait. She had barely finished her course when she got her chance to put her skills to work.

Early in the evening on Saturday, July 5, 1952, Squadron Leader Dick Wynne, the senior medical officer at Sea Island, where Vancouver International Airport is today, was contacted by the RCMP concerning a government surveyor who was seriously injured in a fall on the slopes of Mount Coquitlam. Even though the location was only a few miles northeast of Vancouver, it was in a rugged area where no ambulance could go. Wynne decided to parachute to the accident scene himself, and to take Grace Woodman with him. A man named Red Jamieson would be the jumpmaster on the aircraft.

"From what he had been told, Dick thought the man likely had a punctured lung," Grace recalls. "So we got our supplies together as quickly as we could, climbed into a Dakota, and away we went. We found the general area without too much trouble and did a couple of passes to see where we should jump. The terrain was pretty wild and there didn't seem to be any clear spots. I remember that all you could see for miles were mountain peaks and snow.

"I was quite light — only about a hundred pounds, and I was carrying a couple of kit bags, which weighed sixty pounds or so when I jumped. I had never parachuted from a Dak before, so Dick went first, I followed, and after me, Red. We jumped from about twelve hundred feet.

"Because I was so light, I drifted away from the other two, into a rather isolated area, and I splattered all over the top of a tree. By this time it was starting to get dark."

When Grace Woodman settled into the top of an enormous conifer on the side of the mountain, her chute snagged on some of the topmost branches. The supplies she carried shifted awkwardly, throwing the young woman upside down a few feet closer to the ground. When she stopped crashing through the branches, she was hung up by one leg, hopelessly dangling from the chute harness. At this point, she was about 125 feet high. The weight of the kit was holding her down, trapping her, making it almost impossible to either climb up or go down. Her legs were in pain, her back arched awkwardly, and the gloves she had borrowed just before takeoff fell when she attempted to free herself.

"To top everything off," she explains, "I couldn't get anyone's attention. There was a waterfall fairly close to me, and the roar of the water drowned out my voice. I did yell to Dick and Red, but there was no way they could hear me. By this time, I knew I had to get out of this myself."

For the longest time, the young nurse struggled to free herself. She attempted, again and again, to arch her upper body high enough to undo a snap link that was holding her in the tree. The process was somewhat like doing a sit-up while hanging upside down by one leg. Each time she reached the snap link, the equipment on her back, which she could not release, held her down.

Meanwhile, elsewhere in the bush, Wynne and Jamieson had long since landed and had been calling out and searching for Grace. But as darkness settled, they were forced to wait for first light to continue looking. Sick with worry about their colleague and friend, but realistic enough to know that a search at night would be foolhardy, they located the injured surveyor and began to care for him. Some members of a ground search party had been with him.

"I must have been stuck up that tree for two hours," Grace

continues, "but I finally got myself twisted around and got loose. But getting down was not so great either. I used the rope I had with me to slide down, but without my gloves, and with the extra weight I was carrying, I couldn't control the speed of my descent. The rope was burning into the palms of my hands, and because I was a nurse and needed my hands, I had to make a decision. I decided to chance a broken leg rather than ruin my hands, so I let go of the rope."

When she hit the ground, Grace was certain her leg was broken, but when the pain subsided, she realized it was not. And even though her back hurt, she decided to ignore it and attempt to locate the injured man. She found her gloves, put them on her blood-covered hands, adjusted the kit she carried and started to clamber through the underbrush in the direction she thought the victim lay.

"But after I had gone some distance, I realized I would never be able to reach the others in the darkness," she says. "So I came back to where my chute was and slept under some bushes until morning. I had a jumpsuit on, and a windbreaker, and I wasn't too cold."

The next morning, Grace linked up with Wynne and Jamieson, and helped tend to the man who had fallen. Later in the day, she and the patient at first, and then Wynne and Jamieson, were taken to Vancouver by a U.S. Coast Guard helicopter that had been summoned from Oregon. The injured man survived, and Grace went on with her work. When she got around to removing her gloves after the man had been hospitalized, she realized that their leather had fused itself into the raw flesh on her hands. Eventually, her shredded palms healed, but many decades later, the scars inflicted that night are still readily apparent. The evacuation was all over before Grace even let anyone know about her injuries.

Another mishap, which could have led to several deaths, actually ended on an amusing note. It again involved the Dakota aircraft, a mission of mercy, and a precarious set of circumstances. The person at the centre of the matter was a man named Bill Krier, a now-retired Para Rescue veteran. At the time of the incident he was based at Gander, Newfoundland.

"Every Christmas, we dropped packages to the villages up and down the Labrador coast — Nain, Hopedale, and several others," he says. "But one year, we got a message from an outfit in Montreal who told us they had forgotten to send some cartons of toys to the native kids up in the far northeast, at a place called Wakem Bay. They asked us, if they got the boxes to Goose Bay, could we air drop them. We told them we could, and my sergeant at the time, Carney Hegadorn, sent me to do it.

Bill Krier, left, and Harvey Copeland spent many years in Para Rescue. Both look back on the job with satisfaction — in spite of some unpleasant experiences.

"Anyway, a crewman named Joe Roy and I were in the back of the plane getting ready to do the drop. The stuff had to go out between the peaks of two little mountains, at about 250 feet and at about ninety-five knots. On the first pass, we dropped our streamers, and on the next, we pushed one box out and it went okay. But on the next pass, the damned box jammed going out the door.

"You can't believe the vibration this caused. The old Dak was shaking, the little crewman and I are putting the boots to the box, and the pilot can't figure out what's happening. He thought there was a chute wrapped around the tails so he put on the power and climbed.

"So we pushed and kicked and cursed, and finally the box was freed. The only problem was, when it came loose, it ripped the entire door frame with it. You'd think we dropped the whole side of the airplane. It's minus 45 outside, the plane's wide open, we're wearing parkas and mukluks, and we're still colder than hell. That ten-hour ride home was a long one.

"The one good thing about what had happened was that a couple of months later, we got a letter from a missionary priest up there. He thanked us very much for the Christmas drop, and all the toys — and for the part of our airplane. He wondered though, when we were going to send the rest of it."

For years, the twin-engined Dakota was one of the Search and Rescue workhorses, but when the RCAF received its first helicopter, the Sikorsky S-51, in 1947, the world of SAR in Canada was changed forever. Dutch Franks remembers that "the helicopter allowed us to do a lot of things we had never done before. We could pick up people from crashes and so on that we would not have saved in the past. But the new techniques brought about a lot of improvisation too. For example, when we first started to do stretcher hoisting, we found that a violent thing would happen. As the stretcher rose, the rotor downwash would catch it and it would start spinning. At times, it would fly out to the side on a hundred feet of cable. It was terrible, and it must have been absolutely awful for the patient.

"After I had seen that a couple of times, I decided we had to come up with a better way. At the time, we had all kinds of polypropylene rope, a soft, pink-orange, quarter-inch thing. So I took 150 feet of it, coiled it up, and put a snap on one end. We then tied that to the stretcher. When the engineer sent the stretcher down to us, we simply loaded our patient, tied them on, and then as the stretcher rose, we wood hang onto the rope and feed it out nice and smoothly. Then the stretcher would go up without spinning all over the place. This is still used today."

Another innovation came about with the use of the choppers, this one involving guns.

"I went into a crash once, on a helicopter," Bill Wacey explains. "I was the only Para Rescue guy on board, but there were two Mounties with us. The crash had occurred some time earlier — and because this was in grizzly bear country, we had no idea what we would find. We were not sure if it would be safe at the crash site, so when we got there, and I was going down the hoist, I figured I had better get prepared.

"One of the RCMP guys offered to loan me his gun, a regular police-issue .38 calibre revolver. I didn't think that would do much to a bear, but the other cop had a big .357 magnum, which was his own gun. I told the one guy I didn't want the .38, but that I sure could use the .357. So he gave it to me.

"As it turned out, I didn't need it, because the bears had gone. When I found seven boots with human feet still in them, I sure knew the bears had been there. We hoisted the remains out in a body bag, and then I went up. After that, shotguns became standard equipment on the helicopters."

Para Rescue Specialist Harvey Copeland was also thrilled with the ease with which someone could be lifted from a remote location. But the hoisting did not always go according to plan. He told the author about one incident he will never forget.

"In May 1960, I was stationed at Sea Island. We had been doing a search for a small plane on Vancouver Island, near Nitinat Lake. We found the plane, and a deceased man in it, but the pilot was nowhere around. We assumed he had set out to get help. In order to hoist the victim out, a crew of loggers had to cut down some very tall trees so the helicopter could get low enough. In the meantime, a ground search for the missing pilot was in progress. We searched from the air.

"The ground search was still going on when we were told a man was standing close to where the crash had been, and where we had removed the victim. We flew there, and I was hoisted down into the same rough clearing the loggers had prepared earlier. When I got there, I found one of the ground searchers, a heavy-set young guy, whose knees had given out and he couldn't walk anymore. I got him into a harness and signalled the Flight Engineer to take him up.

"For some reason or other, which neither the engineer nor I knew at the time, the hoist cable started to fray, because it was winding around the drum of the hoist. The young man was maybe seventy or eighty feet in the air, and the cable broke. I still can see him sort of turn over and then fall. He landed flat on his back, with his head hitting one tree trunk and his hips another. There was a terrible sound, and he folded up and went down between the logs. The poor kid didn't have a chance. He was ten feet from me.

"There was nothing more we could do at the time. We were all shaken up, and because we were now without any way to hoist the boy's body, I collected his watch and his wallet and walked out. Word of the death had already been radioed out and by the time I reached Nitinat Lake, there was an RCMP officer there and another man. The man was the boy's father. I handed him the watch and wallet.

"A few days later, the body of the missing pilot was found."

Such incidents of sudden death are familiar to all Para Rescue personnel, or SAR Techs, as they are called today. Copeland and Krier saw the aftermath of many, many crashes over the years, but neither can forget what they didn't see. Bill Krier takes up the story.

"Harv Copeland and I were on a search out of Lac La Ronge, Saskatchewan one terribly hot day in August. This was for a plane with five souls on board that had gone missing at least ten days before. The plane was on floats, and we did find the wreckage. It looked as if the pilot had tried to take off, had hit some trees, and the plane went nose-down into the water.

"That summer, Harv and I had been on a hell of a lot of searches, and it seemed as if we were spending all of our time picking up bodies. On the La Ronge thing, we were in a Twin Otter, and there was another Twin Otter half a mile away, also searching. We knew the SAR Techs in it were young, keen guys who wanted to get another notch or two on their gunbelts. So we called them, told them we were short of gas, and told them where the crash was. We wondered if they would take over. They agreed right away, and we flew back to Lac La Ronge. Half an hour later, we're sitting around, having a beer and telling lies, while the young guys are out there in all that heat, trying to find five left hands, or five skulls or whatever, in order to confirm that all the deceased had been accounted for. Of course, by then, the young guys knew what we'd done."

But thankfully, not all Para Rescue work is so grim. A concluding note from Dutch Franks: "I recall dealing with Bobby Kennedy. He came up to Canada to climb the mountain in the Yukon that was named after John Kennedy. We picked Bobby up in Whitehorse, on a helicopter, and flew him out to Mount Kennedy. The helicopter was stripped down as much as possible, and we flew him as far up the mountain as we could go. We let him out there, and he climbed the rest of the way.

"That was fun for all of us — and for him, I guess."

Dutch Franks, veteran Para Rescue Technician, was instrumental in initiating many of the modifications to equipment used in Search and Rescue today. Mr. Franks was also present when the late U.S. senator Robert Kennedy climbed Mount Kennedy in the Yukon.

2

Tragedy on Baffin Island

I
t was late afternoon when the man returned. He walked
purposefully through the snow along the shoreline, his
head erect, his eyes on the small cabin at the base of the
cliff. In one hand he carried a rifle, still loaded, never fired today
because the seals he had been hunting were nowhere to be seen.
Yet the big man was not disappointed — in fact he was in good
spirits, invigorated by his day-long trek in the clear air of this
lonely land.

To many, Moffet Inlet was really the end of the earth, but
to John Turner, missionary and canon in the Anglican
Church, the dot on the map of Baffin Island was the only
place he wanted to be. After all, he had spent much of the last
eighteen years here, save for a couple holidays in England,
where he had been born, and where he met and married Joan,
the former nursing student who now shared his life. And
despite its hardships, Joan had grown to love the north, while
their daughters, 2-year-old June and 14-month-old Barbara,
knew no other home. And even though it was 450 miles

above the Arctic Circle, the little mission was a place of peace.

Unfortunately, that peace would be shattered on September 24, 1947.

Not far from his destination, Turner caught up with a young Inuit woman named Elizabeth, who was visiting for a few days. Her presence had been a delight for Joan, who now had another adult to talk to, particularly when the constant babble of babies became wearying.

The clergyman greeted his guest and insisted he carry the pail of ice she was lugging to the cabin to melt for drinking water. For a moment the woman protested, but the ice was heavy and her progress had been slow. She smiled shyly, relented, and moved to his side. The two walked and talked as they trudged through the drifts, Turner swinging the pail in one hand and his rifle in the other. The snow crunched underfoot, and the chill of the Arctic dusk was at hand.

Ahead of them, in the Turner cabin, a two-roomed building with an overhead loft and a lean-to at the back, Joan Turner prepared the evening meal. As she did so, the girls played at her feet, their laughter interspersed with occasional spats when both wanted the same toy at the same time. After mediating several of these disputes, Joan was glad her husband would soon be back.

Then she heard his voice.

Outside, Elizabeth stepped back to let Canon Turner open the door. She watched as he switched the pail of ice to his hand holding the gun, while reaching with his other hand for the latch. In that one motion, this 41-year-old man, who was generally so careful, made a terrible mistake. Somehow, the butt of his rifle bumped against the pail as he juggled the two, and the .22 went off.

The bullet hit Turner in the jaw, ripped through flesh and bone, and lodged at the base of his brain. His head snapped back, blood gushed from his face, and he crumpled to the ground. A scarlet stain spread in the snow.

For a second there was utter silence, but then Elizabeth's horrified scream cut the cold. She stumbled backwards, her mind numb, unable to comprehend the enormity of what had just happened. At the same time, Joan Turner opened the cabin door.

Canon Turner lay on his back, his rifle beside him, his face and neck bathed in blood. At first, Joan stared, then, her agony almost too great for words, she dropped to her knees and held the man she loved. He was already unconscious.

Much later, Joan would think back to the day of the accident and would remember the "terrible shrieking" of Elizabeth and the Inuit children who suddenly materialized at the cabin door. They would never forget the sight of the blood, and of their much-loved missionary friend lying in it.

But first, he had to be helped.

In spite of her tears and fears, Joan forced herself to think, to act and to cope. And all the while she prayed as she had never prayed before.

Meanwhile, alerted by the alarm raised by their children, several Inuit adults came running. Each wanted to be of help, in whatever way possible. But before anything else could be done, the stricken cleric had to be moved indoors.

When he was shot, John Turner, who was well over six feet tall, weighed 232 pounds. Because he was too heavy to lift easily, Joan grabbed blankets from the bedroom, laid them beside her husband, and with help, slid them under the injured man's hips and shoulders. Then, as someone held the door, the unconscious Turner was carried inside and laid on the kitchen floor. He still bled profusely.

Despite wanting to remain on her knees beside him, praying aloud and doing her best to stop her husband's bleeding, Joan knew he needed medical attention in the worst way. If he did not get it, he might be dead before morning.

But the nearest doctor was hundreds of miles away; the closest wireless was several hours away by the fastest boat in the area.

The head of an Inuit family offered to go for help. In no time, he had fueled his outboard, tossed an extra container of gas on board and set out for the Hudson's Bay trading post at

Arctic Bay, some seventy-five miles farther north. Most of the trip would be in darkness. In the meantime, Joan did what she could for her husband, while Elizabeth helped with the children.

During that evening, Canon Turner regained consciousness, but because of his injuries, could barely speak. Joan did her best to dress his wounds, but the bleeding continued for several hours, and as it did, the injured man grew weaker and his condition worsened. "I did not think he would live," his wife told a reporter a couple of months later. "I kept him warm. He was conscious and made suggestions."

Joan spent most of that first long, terrible night trying to comfort her husband. She willed him to live and told him he would. She also drew upon her half-forgotten nurse's training in far off England and administered sulpha and other drugs that were among the medical supplies of the mission. In addition to his religious training, John Turner had more than a passing knowledge of pharmaceuticals, and had always insisted that whatever drugs might be needed in an emergency should always be available, no matter how remote the mission. The medicines now being used were ones Turner had brought there himself.

Joan was forced to cut her husband's clothes off, to tend to his sanitary needs, and to feed him — all while he lay on the kitchen floor. After several hours she succeeded in getting him to swallow: first a sip of water, and after that, small amounts of fruit juice. As time went on, only her indomitable spirit kept her going, hours after she was fatigued beyond belief. In the morning, the innocent and delightful solicitation of the children helped see her through.

Finally, on September 28, four days after the accident, a man named John Cormack appeared at the cabin door. He was the Hudson's Bay manager at Arctic Bay, and had been brought by the Inuit trapper who had gone for help. Together, the two built a wooden bed for Canon Turner, and with Joan's help, eased him onto it. Cormack was also able to tell the Turners that he had radioed for help before leaving his post. Now he assured them, probably with more hope than conviction, that all would be well.

*　*　*　*　*

But the appeal had been heard.

Hundreds of miles to the south, at the military base at Rivers, Manitoba, a young army paratrooper named Guy D'Artois was informed about the crisis in the far north. "I was told I would have to make a jump onto Baffin Island," he recalled in an interview years later. "There would be three others with me, but at first no-one really knew many of the details. They came later. I had a feeling though, that this thing might not be easy," he added.

D'Artois was a captain commanding a Special Air Service Force at Rivers at the time of Canon Turner's accident. Prior to that, the Royal 22e Regiment officer from Richmond, Quebec had parachuted at night into occupied France, where he fought the Nazis alongside Resistance personnel. When hostilities in Europe ceased, D'Artois came home wearing the Distinguished Service Order attesting to his heroics. Now, at 31, he was tough, resourceful, experienced, and to those who knew him best, seemingly fearless. If anyone could get Turner out of the north alive, it would be this man. However, D'Artois' premonitions concerning the job would soon become all too real.

The evacuation team assembled at Rivers, but ultimately left from Winnipeg.

Initially, those in charge of what became known as Operation Canon were faced with a host of difficulties. For one thing, it seemed that no-one in Manitoba had any direct knowledge of Moffet Inlet itself, nor did there seem to be any reliable maps of the area. It was only after Reverend M.S. Flint, a former northern missionary, was located in Ottawa that preparations could be solidified. Reverend Flint was flown to Winnipeg and fortunately was able to bring some hand-drawn charts with him. He also had photographs of the isolated mission, which searchers would later use to locate the place from the air.

Finally, on Thursday, October 2, a twin-engine RCAF

transport plane took off from Winnipeg on the mission of mercy. At this point, John Turner had lain injured for eight days.

The first leg of the journey was uneventful. It took pilot Bob Race, D'Artois and the rest of those on board to Churchill, where the plane was serviced and its occupants spent the night. The next day, after some weather-related delays, they continued north by northeast to a settlement called Coral Harbour, a World War II Canadian-American military base on Southampton Island at the northernmost extremity of Hudson Bay. Here, the men continued to work out, as precisely as possible, their plans for the next day, when they hoped to reach their destination.

Assuming that the mission was located without too much difficulty, plans called for four men to parachute to it around noon. The plane would then circle the drop zone as long as fuel supplies and weather permitted, but would go back to Coral Harbour before dark. No-one knew exactly when it would return. Nor did any of the jumpers have any idea how long they would be on the ground. They all knew they would not be able to get out until a suitable landing strip, or a lake frozen solid enough to support the Dak, could be found. Enough food and supplies would be air-dropped to sustain the rescue team for at least a month.

The team consisted of D'Artois, army medical officer Captain Ross Willoughby, who would attend to the needs of Turner, and two Canadian Army signalmen, Sergeants W.W. Judd and H.C. Cook. These two would try to keep in touch with the outside world by radio, while D'Artois would be responsible for selecting the place, time and method of Canon Turner's evacuation. No task would be easy.

It was mid-morning in Coral Harbour when the final part of the trip began. The Dak headed north and located the Turner mission with the help of the charts and photos supplied by Reverend Flint. Before dropping the rescuers, however, the plane flew on to Arctic Bay, where a message was dropped to John Cormack, the Hudson's Bay man. It directed him to find a group of Inuit who could come to Moffet and help transport supplies from the air drop zone to the Turner cabin. Then the plane returned to the area of the mission and the soldiers jumped — although several miles from their target, since the terrain near it was just too formidable.

"At first I was afraid we would never find a safe place," D'Artois told the author. "We flew around and around and there were cliffs, ridges, huge rocks everywhere. Some of the goddamned ridges were probably six hundred feet high. And when we did jump, we were awfully lucky we didn't break our necks. Then we had to get our stuff to the mission." Fortunately, no jumper was disabled.

The Turner cabin was on a sliver of land on the shore of a bay, immediately in front of a cliff. The rescuers set out for it, carrying their heavy equipment, initially cursing the cold but later sweating under their burdens. Today, when we take such things as cellular phones, satellite communication and global positioning capabilities for granted, it is sometimes hard to fathom that in 1947, even transporting a reliable two-way radio was a back-breaking endeavour. And to compound the problem, the main transmitter the signalmen hoped to use was damaged when they located it. A few days later a second was dropped, but the parachute carrying it fell into the sea. Ultimately, parts from a third were cobbled together with the first, and the men carried on.

But the rescuers finally made it to Turner's side. Doctor Ross Willoughby told a reporter what they found. "He was quite conscious when we [first] saw him. He could talk a little, although his words were hard to follow. His left side was complete paralyzed and he was suffering from a gangrenous bed sore ... two inches deep, right to the bone." The doctor described the damage done by the gunshot: "the bullet clipped his upper lip, split the partition of his nose and lodged in his brain." Then Willoughby added, ominously, "just after we got there, I figured that he had lost the will to live."

Yet Canon Turner rallied, fought to survive, and under Willoughby's constant attention and administration of drugs, gradually gained some strength. In the meantime, the other soldiers went about their tasks.

The signalmen painstakingly rebuilt their radio, taking long periods of time to do so. Every time they thought they had a working machine, something malfunctioned and they had to start all over again — all the while using rudimentary equipment, scraps of wires, even tiny strips of metal cut from empty food tins. Then, when they succeeded in making contact with the outside world, weather, atmospheric interference, and mechanical problems elsewhere often ended transmissions prematurely. All the while, the outside world, through relay stations in Churchill, Cambridge Bay, Baker Lake and elsewhere, waited with ever-decreasing faith that Reverend Turner's life would be spared. The longer the delay, it seemed, the worse his chances for survival.

While his colleagues were going about their tasks, D'Artois went to hunt for a suitable landing area so that Race and his crew could make the pickup. Each day, the search took him farther and farther afield. The Inuit helped by suggesting spots, and went to check them out with him, but none were suitable. As his quest widened, D'Artois took provisions, extra clothing, and a tent along and camped on the tundra. At times severe storms shrieked across the desolate landscape, and he had to stay in the tent to wait them out. When he emerged, he looked some more, plodding through snow and coping with almost constant wind and bitter cold. Often, D'Artois drove Inuit dogsleds, but even then the exertion was draining.

As the days passed, the hours of daylight decreased, temperatures dropped, and the smaller lakes started to freeze over. By the beginning of November, the ice would support a man, but this development actually led to another danger.

One morning, D'Artois and David, a young Inuit who was helping him, drove dog teams out onto some solid-looking sea ice. The idea was that if the ice along the shore thickened enough to support a plane, there would be no need to venture farther afield for an inland lake where the Dak could come down. No suitable land area had been found.

Guy D'Artois won the George Medal for his heroic efforts in the rescue of an Anglican clergyman who had been shot at a remote outpost on Baffin Island.

At first, the shore ice seemed promising, so the men stopped to consider their next move. As they did, their teams came close to one another and two dogs started fighting.

The men got them apart, but the team D'Artois drove managed to get its harness impossibly tangled. Then, as he went to sort the mess out, the ice where he stood gave way. The dogs scurried back, but D'Artois plunged into the water and — weighed down by his parka, heavy pants and boots — slipped beneath the surface. By the time he got his bearings he was unbelievably cold, but managed to yell to David to get back or he too would be in the water. Somehow, D'Artois found the strength to roll himself up onto the ice shelf and away from certain death. He stripped to the skin and, shivering uncontrollably, managed, with David's help, to get into some of the dry clothes he had on his sled. The whole episode was over in five minutes.

"I really thought I'd had it," D'Artois said in describing the ordeal. "I was never colder, or more scared. After that little swim, though, I thought I'd better go back and see if the Reverend had any suggestions for me. He knew the land a lot better than I did."

Canon Turner was still far from well, but he was able to tell D'Artois how to get to a lake almost thirty miles away that he thought would be suitable as a landing strip once the ice froze over. That lake, as it turned out, was the one used. D'Artois checked it out and the group waited for freeze-up. Finally, on November 21, almost two months after he was hurt, Canon John Turner was bundled onto a dogsled, transported to the lake, lifted into the waiting Dakota, and airlifted to Stevenson Field in Winnipeg, where an ambulance rushed him to hospital.

He would never return to his beloved Baffin Island.

*   *   *   *   *

Sadly, at 6:30 A.M. on Tuesday, December 8, 1947, Canon Turner passed away at Winnipeg General Hospital. Despite his long and valiant struggle, he never recovered from the gunshot wound inflicted seventy-six days before.

3

Cold War Crash

Late in the evening of March 17, 1953, eighteen American military planes took off from Lagens Airfield in the Azores. Several hours later, seventeen of them reached their destination in Rapid City, South Dakota. The one that did not ended up in thousands of pieces, scattered across a rugged hillside west of Trinity Bay, Newfoundland. Tragically, the bodies of the twenty-three young men who had been on board lay among the ruins. There were no survivors.

The accident happened between 3:51 and 4:00 A.M. on March 18. Sometime during that tiny interval of nine minutes, one of the biggest planes of the early Cold War had ceased to exist. Now, we will never know if it was the fog, the rain, the low ceiling, the plane's inoperable radar, or the fact that it was far off course that ultimately led to the crash. It was likely a combination of the above.

There was some fire; not a lot, but the sound of the crash was heard miles away. In the nearby village of Burgoyne Cove many reported seeing flames, yet later others could not believe they slept through the whole thing. After some delay, the nearest RCMP detachment got the news, and the Mounties alerted the RCAF Search and Rescue unit at Torbay, near St. John's.

The doomed plane was a giant Convair RB-36 strategic/reconnaisance bomber. At the time, no plane was bigger. With ten engines, a wingspan greater than a 747, and incredible range and payload, the machine dominated the skies in its day. Indeed, it was arguably the most important aircraft in the world at the time.

A United States Air Force B-36 bomber flying over Ottawa. This huge aircraft had ten engines, six propeller driven, and pods of two jets on either side. The smaller plane is a Royal Canadian Air Force CF-100 escort. A similar B-36 crashed on a hillside near Trinity Bay, Newfoundland, killing all twenty-three men on board. (Canadian Forces photo)

Originally conceived on an ultra long-range bomb delivery platform for use against the Axis in World War II, the B-36 did not come into service until 1948. By 1953, however, it was an integral component of the U.S. Strategic Air Command. In all, over 300 RB-36s were built, all part of the U.S. arsenal, stockpiled in case of attack from the Soviet Union.

Today, the last such plane that ever flew is in the United States Air Force Museum in Dayton, Ohio. Housed indoors, with several smaller planes actually parked underneath it, the bomber is breathtaking in size — particularly when placed in the context of its time. Because the plane has a wingspan of 230 feet, the building where it is housed had to be built around it. The top of the tail assembly is almost forty-seven feet above the ground.

The aircraft that went down in March 1953 had been the lead plane in the trip across the Atlantic. At the controls that night was Frank Wright, an experienced officer in the U.S. Air Force. A careful and conscientious pilot, Major Wright probably never knew he was off course, or that the nine hundred-foot hillside he hit was in his path. He and the other planes, which followed at fifteen-minute intervals, had crossed the ocean at five hundred feet, deliberately intending to test the capabilities of coastal radar. Had he been on course, Wright's aircraft likely would have proceeded as intended.

The officers and men on the doomed plane were from a variety of towns and cities across the United States. Along with the likes of Lieutenant Edwin Meader of Delaware, Ohio, Airman Burse Vaugh of Evansville, Indiana, and Sergeant Walter Plonski of Scranton, Pennsylvania, was the commanding officer of the Rapid City Air Force Base, Brigadier General R.E. Ellsworth. General Ellsworth's presence on board was confirmed for the press by Lieutenant Robert Baltrano, the public information officer at Rapid City. Ellsworth's name and the names of the other victims were released following notification of next of kin.

Years later, Dick Ellsworth, now a commercial pilot but at the time of the crash a 13-year-old schoolboy, would recall the personal devastation he felt on learning that his father had been killed in an accident. "The day I found out, I had been out delivering my newspapers. When I returned home, I took one look at my mother and asked her what was wrong. I knew by her expression that something was wrong. We only knew then that the

Brigadier General Richard E. Ellsworth, Commanding Officer of Ellsworth Air Force Base, Rapid City, South Dakota. The base was named in General Ellsworth's honour after he was killed in a B-36 bomber crash near Trinity Bay, Newfoundland. (United States Air Force photo)

aircraft had crashed. It was not until later that we knew everyone had been killed." When General Ellsworth died, he also left another son Paul, 11, and a third child, 5-year-old Robert.

Meanwhile, back in Newfoundland, the immediate reaction to the crash was being felt at Torbay. "I was with the 103 Rescue Unit there," explains retired Sergeant Steven Trent. "We were called Para Rescue Specialists in those days, and in the three years I was with 103, we were generally pretty busy. We responded to the B-36 crash as soon as we could."

Trent was 31 years old in 1953, a World War II veteran and a versatile, experienced woodsman who loved jumping from airplanes. He had been a graduate of Canada's first peacetime Para Rescue course.

Also at Torbay then was Joe Coutourier, a tall, dashing, soldier's soldier who hailed from Edmunston, New Brunswick. Sergeant Coutourier, a year or so older than Trent, was also a Para Rescue specialist, and a World War II veteran who had re-enlisted in 1946.

The two made a good team.

"There was a large American presence in Newfoundland in those days," Steve Trent recalls. "But while they had lots of planes, they did not have Para Rescue people at Pepperrell." Pepperrell was a United States Air Force Base near St. John's, operating under the leadership of Colonel Richard Fellows and then part of what the Americans called their Northern Air Command. One of the planes they had in abundance was the venerable DC-3, the Dakota.

Shortly after being asked to help locate the downed bomber, Coutourier and Trent hauled their jump gear aboard U.S.A.F. Dakota 8875 and readied themselves for a search. It was later in the afternoon by the time Major Rich, the aircraft commander, received his clearance from the tower, sped down the runway, and swung west over Trinity Bay. The day was dull and grey and the ceiling no more than a thousand feet. There would be little search time before dark. Coutourier and Trent discussed their intentions.

"We had pretty well worked out how we would handle the whole thing," says Trent today. "I think everyone in our trade tries to think of every scenario imaginable when they are on their way to a crash. I know we did that day. Obviously, you hope and pray there are survivors.

"As soon as we saw the wreckage from the air, though, we knew it would have been an absolute miracle if anyone was alive down there. They must have flown over Random Island on the west side of Trinity Bay, and then tried to get under the weather, but the nose of the plane hit a hill that was about 900 feet high. The plane looked as though it may have flipped. They probably never saw a thing because the hilltop was likely in cloud.

"When we got there, you could see some fire here and there, like oil burning in the snow, but no sign of life. The plane apparently ploughed into the hill and just kept going and going. The wreckage was all over the rocks and scattered for almost a mile. I'll never forget it. I also won't forget flying in there."

When Major Rich sighted the wreckage, he had to take care not to end up like the plane he sought. "There were hills all around us and the clouds were really low by the time we got out there," shudders Trent. "Half the time you couldn't see much. At most, the ceiling was two hundred feet over the crash site so Joe and I knew we could never jump there. By then, we really wanted to get the hell out of the Dak though, before we crashed into something ourselves."

It was now almost dark.

A quarter of a mile below the wreckage, and off to one side, Coutourier noticed the white, snow-covered ice surface of a small lake.

"The top of the hill was scrubby forest," Trent remembers, "but down by the lake, the trees were twenty-five to thirty feet high. We decided we would try for the lake. At that point, we had no idea how deep the snow was. The pilot flew between hills to get us there.

"We had to jump from about seven hundred feet, because if you went any higher, you couldn't see the ground. Luckily our chutes opened because there was sure no time for a backup.

"Joe went first, but because I was a little heavier in those days, I came down first," Trent continues. "I went into the bush and got hung up in the trees for a while. Joe was luckier. He went through them onto the ground."

Because of the deep snow and the approaching darkness, the two men knew it would be impossible to climb to the crash site before morning. They had no radio contact with either the Dak or with their own base in those days, so they were relieved when they got a glimpse of the aircraft as it reappeared overhead. As it passed, a tent, sleeping bags and rations were dropped. Then, after the engines died in the distance, Trent and Coutourier shouted for several minutes in the direction of the crash site. When their entreaties went unanswered, they prepared for a night in the snow.

"We were up and ready to go at dawn," Sergeant Trent recalls. "And it was a tough climb up that hill. Fortunately, we were wearing snowshoes, because without them we would have sunk to our waists."

The trek up the face of the steep hillside, coping with the snow, carrying heavy packs, and clambering through the underbrush, took the men ninety minutes, half as long as it takes hikers today in the summer.

"We really pushed ourselves," says Trent, "because even though we were almost certain no one was alive up there, we kept hoping."

Once they reached the crash, the tangle of devastation and the broken bodies of the dead men seemed to be everywhere. For Trent, the mission was his first involving loss of life — so it is no wonder the things he saw have remained vivid in his mind to this day.

"We knew the Americans would be coming in with a coroner, so we marked the locations of the victims, but didn't disturb their remains in any way. After we located all we could, we began picking up and securing classified papers that were lying all over the place. These meant nothing to us."

During the morning, two men from the local area arrived on the scene. They had been cutting wood down at the base of the hill and had climbed up to see if they could be of assistance. One of them picked up an altimeter as a souvenir but was cautioned by Coutourier and Trent about removing it. Both knew the instrument could prove vital in the crash investigation which would necessarily follow. The woodcutters were otherwise very useful in helping to mark the location of bodies and retrieving the scattered documents.

Steve Trent, former Para Rescue
Specialist who parachuted to the B-36
crash in Newfoundland

*   *   *   *   *

There were four sequels to the story of the B-36 crash.

Another American aircraft, in this case a smaller B-29 bomber with ten souls on board, crashed into St. George's Bay, Newfoundland while searching for the wreckage of the first plane. Again, no-one survived, so a total of thirty-three young men died on that one terrible day in 1953.

The second development resulting from the tragedy was played out more than half a continent away, at Rapid City. Here, at the intended destination of the eighteen planes that had left the Azores that long-ago March evening, Dwight Eisenhower, president of the United States at the time, officially renamed the South Dakota military compound after its commander, who had been on board the ill-fated aircraft. As the General's widow Mary Anne stood with tears in her eyes on the platform behind him, the president officially proclaimed that from then on, the

Memorial services at Rapid City, South Dakota for the victims of the B-36 bomber crash in Newfoundland in March, 1953. The aircraft in the background is similar to the one lost. (United States Air Force photo courtesy Dick Ellsworth)

United States president Dwight Eisenhower addresses the crowd in 1953 during the dedication ceremonies for Ellsworth Air Force Base at Rapid City, South Dakota. Mary Anne Ellsworth is standing behind the President, and 13-year-old Dick Ellsworth is at the left of the photo. (United States Air Force photo courtesy Dick Ellsworth)

facility would be known as Ellsworth Air Force Base. It is still operational today.

Thirdly, on May 17, 1954, fourteen months after the crash, Steve Trent and Joe Coutourier were involved in something far more pleasant than attempting to reach a downed plane. At U.S. Armed Forces Day at Pepperrell Air Force Base, thousands of Newfoundlanders came to watch as Lieutenant-General Charles T. Myers, commander-in-chief of the United States Northeast Command, invited the two young Canadians to the reviewing stand on the parade square. There, in front of the visitors and the massed squadrons of American Air Force personnel, General Myers cited Trent and Coutourier for parachuting to the B-36 crash. He then conferred upon them the U .S. Soldier's Medal for heroism, the citation for which read, in part, "with complete disregard for their own safety, they unhesitatingly accepted the personal risk and performed the jump even though aware of the fact that the altitude precluded use of their emergency parachutes if the primaries malfunctioned.

"The courage, perseverance and devotion to duty displayed by Sergeants Trent and Coutourier reflect great credit upon themselves, the Royal Canadian Air Force and Canada."

And lastly, forty years after the crash, a group of flight engineers and others at 103 Rescue Unit in Newfoundland came up with a plan to honour the memory of the deceased airmen. They decided to erect a monument on the crash site, if possible including a propeller from the lost plane. Author and participant Mark Marchant described the difficulties involved: "The wreckage was spread over a large area in rough terrain: on bald rock, through thick forest, over steep hills, and in boggy valleys. Nine blades were eventually located out of a total of eighteen. It took seven men to move the least damaged to an area where it could be extricated by helicopter."

The blade was refurbished, a verse from the Bible was inscribed on it, and then the relic was mounted on a concrete pedestal and left to mark the crash site. A plaque bearing the names of the twenty-three men who died on that spot was affixed to the base of the structure.

On August 3, 1993, Steve Trent and Joe Coutourier unveiled the memorial. It stands on that hilltop today, for all the world to see. It is indeed a tribute to the men who died, but also to the courage of the two who risked their lives to help.

Their actions, though unsuccessful in saving lives, were appreciated by the relatives of those who died. In letters to Trent and Coutourier dated December 11, 1953, Mary Anne Ellsworth expressed her thanks in a brief but poignant manner: "It was only recently I learned of your courageous jump last March 18, and with all my heart I wish a different scene had met your eyes. I am most sincerely grateful. God bless you for trying — no man can do more."

To Trent and Coutourier, her words meant more than any medal.

4

Smashed Up, Sucked Down, Destroyed

One rainy morning in April 1971, a farmer named Peter Blackburn walked into a field by his barn, near St. Jean Vianney, Quebec, to see what was bothering his cows. The herd had been grazing quietly until all at once it began to shy away from a particular spot. Then the cows stampeded to a far fence and remained there, obviously agitated. They stared dumbly as Blackburn appeared.

A minute or so later, it was Blackburn who stared — but not at his cattle.

He had gone less than a hundred yards when he saw something he would never forget.

There, in front of him, in what had been a flat, ordinary-looking pasture field, was a gaping hole in the ground, several feet across, and so deep he couldn't see the bottom.

Blackburn stepped back mesmerized, barely comprehending. Then he inched forward, peered into the pit and wondered just what in hell this was. He looked and looked, rooted to the spot, mystified, bewildered, and then alarmed — he feared his cattle could blunder into the hole before he could get them all into his barn. He would worry about the cause of the pit later.

Blackburn saved his cattle and reported the hole in the field to the local officials, and they in turn contacted provincial authorities. Several theories as to what brought about this wonder were cited, but apart from determining that it was some kind of a sinkhole, and that it was at least 150 feet deep, no-one could supply any firm answers as to its origin. All that most people who came to look at the hole knew was that the junk they threw into it took a long time to hit bottom.

*   *   *   *   *

That same spring, the National Hockey League playoffs were held — as usual. In Quebec, the fortunes of the Montreal Canadiens and their attempts to win the Stanley Cup were followed widely — as usual. There was a hockey game on television on the night of Tuesday, May 4; the game was in Chicago, between the Habs and the Black Hawks. Chicago won that night, 2–1 in overtime, but Montreal would ultimately take the Cup in seven games.

The May 4 game was typical, hard-fought playoff hockey, with the winner not decided until the final second. For that reason, virtually every hockey fan in Quebec was still up, watching television at 11:00 P.M.

This was certainly the case in St. Jean Vianney, the town near Peter Blackburn's farm.

Slightly over one hundred miles north of Quebec City, and ten miles from Chicoutimi, St. Jean Vianney was at the confluence of two rivers, the mighty Saguenay and the tiny, eight-foot-wide Riviere aux Vases, or "River of Mud." In 1971, about 1,300 people lived there. Most worked at area mills, and particularly at the Aluminum Company of Canada operation in nearby Arvida. And while the town may not have been an oasis of opulence, it was a comfortable, middle-class bedroom community like scores of others across the province.

But not for long.

Suddenly, residents of St. Jean Vianney felt their houses shake. At first slightly, then stronger. Hanging lights swung, televisions flickered, and in many cases, family dogs yelped. Crashing sounds were heard in the streets.

People ran outside and couldn't believe what they saw.

Their quiet little community had become the monstrous centre of hell.

Up and down the streets, entire houses were moving, breaking apart, falling in on themselves and disappearing. Parked cars and trucks were upended and gone as roads and the driveways leading to them vanished. Street lamps swung in the wild rain, then quickly went out in showers of sparks as the poles that held them crashed to the ground.

Then there were screams: loud, wailing, wrenching cries of terror out of the darkness. From here, there, a block away, and from right next door. Calls for help, sobs, moans, curses and half-heard prayers in the night. At first close by, then farther and farther away. Cries of the young, the old, the infirm and the fit, who were all dying. Dying in terrible ways, in a hideous cataclysm they neither anticipated nor understood. Dying as sure as their town was dying around them.

And still, no-one knew what was happening.

Hockey fan Jean-Paul Boivin would later remember the shaking of his home. Alarmed, he dashed outside and there, as dozens of screaming people in nightclothes stood transfixed, watched a neighbour's house break apart and disappear.

He sprinted back inside, gathered his wife and their four children together and led them into the street. When the six had gone less than a hundred yards, he glanced over his shoulder in time to see their home crash down and sink from sight. He was thankful to be safe, but too scared to cry.

In another case, a block away, a man was getting ready for bed when his house began to shake and he heard a rumbling outside. He went to investigate, but he was barely off the doorstep when his house vanished behind him. Inside it were his wife, Rosa Brassard, and their 15-day-old daughter, who had been baptized only hours before. Neither was seen again; nor was the Brassard home.

Roger Landry had gone to his basement for something when he felt the cement floor tremble under his feet. He immediately forgot what he wanted, and instead turned to the stairs and raced up — two at a time. By this time, his house was already half destroyed, and his family wasn't there. He frantically climbed through what had been the kitchen, screamed for his wife, and in a blind panic tore away rubble leading to their bedroom.

To no avail.

Seconds later, as the remains of his house slid out from under him, he dived for the door. In that instant, the house was gone, and with it Landry's world. His wife and their five children — Jeannette, 21, Helene, 17, Anna, 16, Denis, 15, and Bruno, 13 — all died that night.

"I called them until I thought my lungs would burst," he said later, "but there was no answer. It was dreadful, indescribable." Landry searched in vain, for hours and hours, but at last, utterly desolate, accepted an offer of shelter from relatives.

Another St. Jean Vianney resident survived the catastrophe, along with her husband and their ten children, but only because of a combination of dogged persistence, selfless courage, and a mother's love that knew no bounds.

Like Roger Landry, Mrs. Marcel Boily had been in the basement when the earth tremors began. She had just returned from a hospital stay, and was up late doing some of the laundry that had piled up while she was away. The washing complete, she gathered a bundle of clean clothes and was bringing them up from the basement when the stairs shook and she heard a racket outside.

She dropped what she carried and went to the door.

People outside were screaming and crying, yelling for those in their houses to get out because the street was collapsing. Mrs. Boily left the door open, then ran and awakened her family and

Houses break up after falling into a sink hole in St. Jean Vianney, Quebec after the devastating disaster in 1971. (Photo by Mel Furlotte)

quickly led them from the house. "We raced up Harvey Street in our bare feet," she told the *Montreal Star* in a story carried on May 8, 1971, four days after her escape. "People were screaming frantically and shoving each other as the ground kept shaking. I saw one person fall down and disappear."

When she reached the top of a hill, Mrs. Boily noticed that her 12-year-old son, who had been sick in bed all day with a fever, was not there. Telling everyone to stay put, she ran back down the street to rescue him. A policeman who arrived on the scene tried to block her path.

"I pushed him away and ran, but he caught up to me and grabbed me. I struggled with him and tried to tell him about my son, but he wouldn't listen, so I began hitting him," she said.

During the struggle both fell to the ground, but Mrs. Boily managed to free herself and run off. As she entered her house, she heard a loud roar and watched with horror as her neighbours' house slid away.

"I was so scared, I couldn't remember at first where my son's room was," said Mrs. Boily. After finding him, she picked him up and carried him out. As she reached the end of the driveway, the ground shook again and she caught a glimpse of her house disappearing.

Stopping momentarily to look at the gaping hole where the house she and her husband had saved for over many years had stood, Mrs. Boily felt someone pulling at her arm and turned around to see the same police officer who had earlier attempted to stop her.

Together they ran to safety and joined the rest of her family.

In another area of St. Jean Vianney, a bus carrying workers home from the Arvida aluminum plant was making its way along an outlying street. Because of the extremely heavy rain and poor visibility, driver Jules Girard was proceeding with a great deal of caution. He would later claim that this caution saved his life and the life of everyone on the vehicle. His passengers, all of them, readily agreed.

Girard's bus was creeping along in second gear, its driver hunched over the wheel as he tried to see through sheets of rain. The windshield wipers slapped to and fro, but they didn't help much. Nor did the headlights; they were reflected by the rain, and made it even harder to see.

But then Girard realized he wasn't seeing *anything*.

His lights shone into space: there was no white line, no shoulder and, it seemed, not even a road out there!

He hit the brakes.

Behind him, half a dozen lunch buckets fell on the floor and clattered up the aisle, and the passengers lurched forward as the bus halted. All conversation stopped.

For a few seconds, no-one moved. All eyes were on the front — where there was nothing to see.

Girard peered into the blackness, then opened the door, thinking he would get out and check the road.

But at this point, the front of the bus dropped.

This prompted an immediate, wild scramble to the back of

the vehicle. Somebody opened the emergency door, and in no time, every passenger was outside. Girard was the last to leave.

Seconds later, the earth collapsed under it and the bus tumbled end over end, down out of sight. The men who had just been in it didn't even notice the rain.

* * * * *

Sometime shortly after midnight, during the unfolding of the disaster at St. Jean Vianney, a telephone rang at the Canadian Forces Base at Bagotville, twenty-eight miles southeast. The information relayed was jumbled, incomplete and barely believable. The caller wanted help right away because a town was disappearing and a lot of people were dying. Few other details were forthcoming.

"When we got the message from RCC [Rescue Co-ordination Centre] we didn't know what to think," recalls Mel Furlotte, a flight engineer with Bagotville Search and Rescue at

Rod Verchere risked his life, several times, to search for possible landslide victims in the Saguenay region of Quebec in 1971. Flight engineer Mel Furlotte was in the helicopter with Verchere.

the time. "They told us virtually nothing, just to have a helicopter ready to go right away, and to put a couple of extra stretchers in it. We had no idea where we were going, or why.

"We had been watching the hockey," he continues, "and boy, was I happy to see Chicago win! I hated the Canadiens. Anyway, we forgot about the game and got the plane ready. We were airborne in less than an hour.

"By the time the helicopter left Bagotville, further messages that had come in mentioned a landslide in a little town called St. Jean Vianney. None of us knew quite where it was, but we knew it had to be to the north, somewhere around the Shipshaw Dam. We'd seen the dam from the air on lots of occasions. In the meantime, the weather is terrible. There's fog, rain and high winds. We're in the most useless helicopter in the world, and we don't know where we're going. Fun, eh?"

An Air Force helicopter, the so-called "flying banana", hovers above the remnants of a house in the muddy sink hole at St. Jean Vianney. (Canadian Forces photo by Manny Soberall)

The helicopter in question was the Vertol H-21, called the "flying banana" because of its long, curved shape. The machine was difficult to fly, underpowered, undependable, and prone to stalling. In fact, a few months earlier, Furlotte and his entire crew had crashed in an identical machine because of a power failure at a critical time. Ron Servos, the second flight engineer, had spent several weeks in the hospital recovering from injuries.

"So none of us were super-confident about things," Furlotte adds, "but luckily the guys up front were the best in the business." They were Palmer "Tiny" Wenaas and Jack Farncombe, the two pilots.

"We followed the highway up past Arvida," Furlotte says, "and you could hardly see a damned thing as we went along. Then we found the Shipshaw Dam somehow and figured where we were going was somewhere close by. There were no lights though, and we didn't know then that all the power was out in St. Jean Vianney.

"Finally we saw some flashing lights from police cars, so we landed and asked what was going on. They told us that right out in front of us there were no roads, no houses, no trees, or anything else. They said there had been a landslide and everything had gone down into it.

"So we took off and found the hole.

"It was the most monstrous thing I had ever seen. We could see houses falling over the side, smashing up, being sucked down and being totally destroyed. There was lumber, bathtubs, cars, the sides of buildings — you name it — floating away. It was absolutely stupendous. And we didn't know then how big it was.

"Tiny decided to fly around the circumference to see if we could find anyone alive down inside. At this time, we had no SAR Techs on board, only Ron and I in the back. Ron was at the front right door, and I was at the back, looking out the left side.

"We had only a single light — a landing light — but it was not much good. The damned thing was a piece of junk, and it would only work for about five minutes at a time, then it would blow a relay switch and go out. Every time that happened, we would fly out of the hole so that at least we were over firm ground if the engine quit.

"We went back and forth, down in the pit, trying to locate

anyone who might have been alive. The whole thing was so eerie. In the darkness and rain, you really could not tell how awesome it was. We would come over the edge, then go down and hover, just above the moving mud. None of us had a lot of faith in the helicopter, and we knew if we stalled, we would never get out. There just wasn't anyone alive down there that we could see. It was a terrible place. We kept searching until about 3:30 and found no-one. By then we needed gas so we decided to go back to the base and wait for morning so that we could see. I remember being exhausted by the time we left."

As soon as the H-21 had landed in Bagotville the ground crew checked it over and made sure it would be ready when the operation resumed at dawn. The four fliers grabbed an abbreviated rest, but by 6:30 A.M. they were back in the aircraft, awaiting takeoff clearance from the tower. This time, Para Rescue specialist Rod Verchere went with them.

A former farmboy, Verchere grew up near Mission City, British Columbia. He had hunted, fished, and played every sport around prior to going to Vancouver at 18, intending to join the navy. He went to the air force instead, and tells anyone who will listen that it was one of the best decisions he ever made. An engaging man, with a quick, dry wit, he quickly acquired and earned a reputation for being totally fearless, particularly in his Para Rescue work. Undoubtedly, he was the right person at the right time at St. Jean Vianney. His action there won him the Star of Courage, Canada's second-highest award for bravery. He certainly earned the decoration.

"He is probably the most dedicated person I've ever met," enthuses Mel Furlotte. "He's afraid of nothing, and would do anything, anywhere, if he felt there was even a remote chance of saving a life. He went into situations that were terrifying and operated with a complete disregard for his own safety. I know if I was in trouble, I would be damned thankful to see him. That was why we were lucky to have him with us in the pit."

Once airborne, the chopper followed the Saguenay north. While the weather had improved slightly, it was still drizzling and the clouds were dark. Below the plane, the river looked placid in the early dawn. It was clear and clean, until they got closer to their destination.

"I remember looking over one of the pilot's shoulders," recalls Mel Furlotte, "and noticing how the river suddenly became very muddy. Then a bit farther along, it was clear again. That's when we noticed a stream of silt coming in from the right side, with all this junk floating out on it. Until that moment, we had not connected the big pit at St. Jean Vianney with this runoff into the Saguenay. But there it was."

What had been the tiny Riviere aux Vases was now an ugly hundred-foot-wide moving mass of debris-choked brown water and mud. It came from inland, and about a mile further along, flowed from the enormous sinkhole that had shattered the lives of so many the night before.

The rescue helicopter had just turned inland from the Saguenay when someone noticed a corpse entrapped in the slime below.

"We went down," says Furlotte, "and then swung in over the body, a man. By the time we got him out of there and had the body in a bag, we had mud to our hips. The stuff was like thick, grey soup that moved."

The deceased was taken to a nearby emergency measures centre, and the chopper flew on to the sinkhole itself.

"When I first saw it, I couldn't comprehend the enormity," says Rod Verchere. "It was so vast, and so unbelievable, I thought there would be hundreds dead down there. It was more or less about a half-mile across, and two hundred feet deep, and there were lots of houses and parts of houses down inside. Some others were still falling off the cliff, and this was six or seven hours after the slide started.

"The scope of the disaster and how long a goddamned day this was going to be were two thoughts running through my mind. I also knew we had to make a plan pretty quick, because this was unlike anything any of us had seen before."

Shortly after their arrival over the enormous sinkhole, the

helicopter crew located a car down in the bottom, but not far from one side. A woman clung to its roof in desperation, fearful that at any moment the wreck would shift and she would be sucked into the morass that surrounded her. Far above, on the rim of the pit, would-be rescuers saw her but dared not climb down to help. They knew that doing so would mean certain death.

"We lifted her out of there," recalls Mel Furlotte. "Rod was in a wetsuit and he got a horsecollar around her. She had been there all night, yelling for help and when we arrived, she was shaking and crying, but could not speak. Her voice had completely gone. She had a few bruises, but was in fairly good shape otherwise. We learned later that her name was Lisette Lepine."

Farcombe, Wenaas and the H-21 crew then began a systematic search of the hole, concentrating initially on what remained of the houses that were deep inside.

"We would hover over a house," explains Furlotte, "and if the pilots could get one of the back wheels on something solid, a roof, or a porch, or something like that, Rod would hop out and go inside. In all, he checked seven or eight, but we found no-one. When he came out, we would haul him up."

Verchere often had trouble making his way through what remained of the buildings he entered. Sometimes a jammed door had to be kicked open, or broken-down partitions inside had to be clambered over. Yet every room was checked. In all cases, the layout of the house was unfamiliar, there were no lights, and upturned beds, refrigerators, sofas and the remnants of televisions were sometimes piled in a shambles together. Just getting over the junk, checking under it, and slithering through broken glass to get to the various rooms took time. And all the while, the buildings were moving, their roofs and walls were collapsing, creating an ever-present danger of being trapped.

"I felt like a break-and-enter artist," Verchere laughs, "but these places were the end of somebody's dreams. I didn't know when I would stumble over a body, or exactly what I would find. There were still some homes coming down from on top, but we knew the people had cleared out of them.

"I remember later, a reporter from the *Toronto Star* asking me if I had kids. I told him I had, and he asked where they were.

"I said, 'Right there,' and I pointed over the Arvida school, a half-mile away. Then he wanted to know if I was thinking of my kids when I was going through the houses. I said, hell no, the only kids I was thinking about were the ones who might have been down in the pit. I told him I was mainly thinking of how to get my ass out of the hole. That ended the interview."

As Verchere was going into each house, the chopper hovered above, the crew watching from their vantage point. Mel Furlotte remembers, "we would go to perhaps a hundred feet and wait, as the buildings moved along and fell in on themselves. Rod would be gone for the longest time, but then he'd come out; we would pull him up and take him to the next. A couple of times, he wasn't coming out and the house was falling apart, and we would be sure he was gone, that the poor bugger was dead for sure. Then he'd pop out, give a thumbs up, and we'd hoist.

"During all this time we were more scared for him than he was. Finally we told him "Enough. No more.' Then, 'In a minute,' he'd say. 'Let me down over there. I want to check that one.' He kept doing that until we had to leave for fuel. When we got back there were no more houses."

"We then looked for cars, things like that," Verchere goes on. "I'd get hoisted down in order to check each one we found. They were all empty. After that, it was mostly picking up bodies."

Late in the afternoon, when the primary recovery work was done, Wenaas put the chopper down near a police command post. He and his men were wrung out, exhausted, and long past the end of their crew day. No-one was more tired than Rod Verchere.

"I had been handling bodies; I was covered in mud, and I was so beat I could hardly move," he says, "so I lay down in my wetsuit on a big rock.

"About five minutes later, a wing commander from Bagotville walked up to me and told me the general was there from Valcartier, and he wanted to see me. I told him that as far as I was concerned, if the general wanted to talk to me, he could come and speak to me. I was too tired to move.

"Hell, the next thing I knew, this big six-foot-six-inch guy was standing beside me. It was General St. John — the Army General. I started to scramble to my feet when I saw him but he said 'No, stay where you are.' He picked a rock, sat down and we had a chat. He asked me what I thought of the whole situation and I told him. Then he asked me how I liked Bagotville. I told him I didn't like Bagotville, that I was a Para Rescue man and I should be in Trenton or somewhere where there was a regular Para Rescue outfit.

"Ten days later I was in Trenton."

One of many smashed houses lies at the bottom of the sink hole. (Canadian Forces photo by Manny Soberall)

*   *   *   *   *

For several days, cleanup continued at St. Jean Vianney and along the Riviere aux Vases and the Saguenay. In all, thirty-one people were killed in the catastrophe, fourteen of them children.

Thirty-six homes were completely destroyed, as were several cars, one bus, and an unknown number of family pets. Almost two thousand people were evacuated to safer places, and some fifteen million tons of mud and earth were displaced.

There were hundreds of stories of hardship, self-sacrifice, heroism and loss. One of the most pathetic involved a man whose son, his pregnant daughter-in-law, and his little granddaughter had all been killed. Four days after their deaths had been confirmed, the grieving gentleman appeared at a relief centre to get clothes for them. He was unable to accept the fact that they were gone forever.

A worker at the centre led him gently away.

*   *   *   *   *

And the cause of the disaster? The experts blamed several days of rain, a possible underground stream, unstable clay, and shifting water-soaked soil that had been there since the last Ice Age. Many others, of course, just blamed the government. One of those was Peter Blackburn, the farmer with the hole in his field. That hole, almost beside the main cave-in at St. Jean Vianney, was a precursor of the disaster — and a warning. If the politicians of the day had reacted to the destructive power of the first cave in and evacuated people, many lives would have been saved.

After all, Blackburn's cattle had certainly moved back.

5

Rescue Shock

Hans Hauer was a dreamer. He dreamed of becoming a pilot, so he took lessons and got his wings. Later, he dreamed of owning a plane, so he checked what was available and bought a little two-seater. Then he dreamed of flying away — far away, beyond his home town, his home province, even beyond his home country. In fact, Hans Hauer dreamed of flying his Cessna 150 across the northern Atlantic Ocean. But in early July 1972, his dreams died.

Luckily, he did not die with them.

Hauer had spent long periods of time making plans that would take him from Nanaimo, British Columbia to Germany. He acquired the necessary maps; he noted the patterns of weather en route; he estimated times, distances, and probable landing sites along the way, and he convinced himself that he could cope with any emergencies he might encounter. Then he turned to the little white plane that would make his dreams come true.

Because he knew he could never hope to traverse miles and miles of open sea with the gas the Cessna ordinarily carried, Hauer reconfigured the on-board supply by installing several jerrycans of fuel, along with plastic tubes to feed it. Then, convinced that the plane was mechanically sound, he loaded it with good food, said goodbye to family and friends and departed Nanaimo.

He was 55 years old at the time.

Hauer's route took him out of B.C., over the Rocky Mountains, across the prairies, and then northeast — above the northern tip of Hudson Bay to the Southampton Island town of Coral Harbour.

That was as close to Germany as he got.

When the pilot walked into the air terminal at Coral to file a flight plan he encountered what, to his disappointment, was an insurmountable obstacle. The little Cessna lacked the proper navigational aids for a trans-Atlantic flight. Hauer knew his journey to Germany was over; he turned back.

Late in the evening of July 2, Hauer flew southward, along the Hudson Bay coast towards Churchill, Manitoba, where he intended to refuel. Somehow, in the darkness, he either could not locate the town, or he ran out of gas, or both. When he did not arrive when expected, a search was launched for him.

The Rescue Co-ordination Centre in Edmonton received the call for help, and a Hercules transport aircraft from 435 Squadron responded. There were two SAR Techs on board the plane, both of whom were from 440 Squadron. Pete Howard and George Walker were corporals at the time, and this was their first mission together as team leaders. Because one had to be designated jumpmaster, they flipped a coin to see who that would be, and Howard won. The pilot on the mission was Captain Graham and the Herc he flew was Number 326.

Pete Howard remembers the fight from Edmonton to Churchill as being long and extremely boring. Finally however, several hours after their departure from Alberta, the crewmen found themselves looking out over Hudson Bay. At that point, the search really began.

Pete Howard took the initiative in starting intravenous therapy in order to save the life of a plane crash victim in northern Manitoba. At the time, SAR Techs could not start an IV without medical supervision. Because of Howard's actions, this rule was changed.

"It took us so damned long to get there," says Howard today, "that we were tired before we started. We went into our search pattern, over the tundra, where we knew millions of mosquitoes waited if we had to jump. It was quite hot, as I recall," he adds.

The search ended almost as soon as it started.

"We were six and a half hours getting to Churchill," Howard explains, "and then George found the crash right away — in less than ten minutes. We were incredibly lucky, because there were no ELTs [Emergency Locator Transmitters] in those days. You either found a crash or you didn't. You had to see it, and we saw this one.

"We flew low over the site, but there was no one around. It looked as if the guy tried to land, but the muskeg was so soft, he flipped over. He was about thirty miles from Churchill, close to the Knife River. As far as we could tell from the air, the plane was reasonably intact, and had not burned.

"But God, it was windy. We considered the situation very carefully because of the wind. But after three or four low passes over the site, and we had not seen any sign of life, we decided we should go, high winds or not. In situations like this, the pilot, who is in control of the aircraft, cannot say, 'You *will* go.' He could only have told us that we could *not* go. Anyway, we told the front end that because the guy wasn't coming out, he could be lying there injured, so we couldn't just fly away. We had to go down and look. Captain Graham agreed."

Both SAR Techs were well aware of the danger as they strapped on their parachutes. Once ready, they checked each other's equipment and stood by as the big ramp at the rear of the plane was lowered. The loadmaster dropped a couple of streamers to assess the wind speed, and these blew far across the green wastes below. When it came time for the men to jump, they gave each other a thumbs-up sign, and away they went.

"At least it was wide open around there," Howard says. "You could see for miles and miles, and we kept the crash in sight as we steered towards it. Our parachutes in those days had a ten miles per hour maximum forward speed, so driving into the wind made it seem as if we were going backwards at twice that. And because of the wind, we both knew we could easily be hurt when we landed, but luckily we weren't."

Both jumpers landed fairly close together, but just as he was about to touch, Howard hit a boot-high hummock when he began to do a parachute roll. The little bump knocked his feet out from under him and he fell flat on his back. The shock winded him, but he managed to scramble to his feet and began to gather in his chute. Walker was already prepared to go on. Gear from the plane above them had been dropped about hundred yards or so from the crash. The SAR Techs collected it and prepared to walk to their objective. There was still no sign of life.

"Then we broke the first rule of Search and Rescue," Howard admits today, rather sheepishly. "Instead of calling out in the direction of the crash, and announcing our presence, we just walked over to it. We should have been yelling, 'Mr . Hauer, are you alright?' or something to that effect, but for some reason or other, we didn't. And I really don't know why not."

The failure of the SAR Techs to signal their approach had an obvious effect on the downed pilot.

Hans Hauer had survived the crash of his plane. He had indeed attempted a landing on the tundra, but because of the surface softness, the wheels of the aircraft sank into the muskeg, causing the Cessna to nose forward and flip onto its roof. For some unknown reason, Mr. Hauer was not wearing a seatbelt, so the impact of the crash tossed him around the cabin, leaving him lying in pain, unable to move his lower body at all. The crash had occurred some twelve hours prior to the arrival of the SAR Techs, and the injured man suffered where he lay.

"Then I clumped up to the plane, stuck my head inside and asked 'Are you okay Mr. Hauer?'" recalls Pete Howard. "Good God, it's lucky the shock of my arrival didn't kill him. The poor guy has been lying there for hours, he hasn't heard our aircraft, but he does hear something outside. He did hear the two thumps when we landed, the thump of our equipment, then the thump, thump, thump as we came closer. He's sure there are bears out there and he can't move and they're coming closer. Then I stick my head in and start yelling right beside him. No wonder the guy was terrified. His eyes were the size of saucers. He was pretty glad to see us though."

While Howard set about doing everything he could for the injured man, George Walker contacted the circling Herc and described the situation on the ground. He reported that the downed pilot was alive but badly injured, and that a helicopter would be required in order to get him to a hospital. The message was acknowledged.

"I did a quick check of his vitals," said Peter Howard, "but he was in pretty rough shape. Fortunately, he was a big, robust, strong man, and perhaps that's why he was still alive. And even though he was just lying there, unable to help himself otherwise, he had a strength of will that was remarkable — or at least was until we got there. At first he was alert, answered our questions, told us what had happened and so on.

"As I worked on him, I knew his back was broken because

he had no feeling from the nipple line down. His bladder was distended because he had been unable to urinate, and I figured his pelvis was fractured. But then I noticed that the alertness was gone.

"He went into what might be called rescue shock. He had held on so long alone, fighting to stay alive. However, now that we were there, he relaxed, thinking he was now okay. That was a big mistake. The poor guy started babbling and wasn't making any sense at all. I did a carotid artery check and I couldn't feel any pulse. Then I couldn't get a pulse on his wrist either. When he was fighting to stay alive, there was muscle tension and he was helping himself. Now however....

"As I saw him sink lower and lower I knew we were going to lose him unless I did something pretty damned quick. Until that time, SAR Techs were not permitted to start IVs in the field unless a doctor was present, or at least gave permission for the procedure. Since there was no doctor around, and none there to ask, and we had a dying man on our hands, I decided to go ahead and start the intravenous anyway.

"Then I remember saying to George, 'Call the aircraft. Tell them to call Churchill. Tell them I cannot get a carotid pulse on this guy. Tell them I need permission to start an IV. Then pretend their answer is garbled and ignore it — don't pay any attention to what they say because I'm going to do it anyway. We can't wait for permission.'

"George says 'Right on!'

"Then I asked Mr. Hauer for permission. He sort of said 'yeah' and I started the IV. Then George called.

"Mr. Hauer seemed to react right away. He got major colour and was more alert. By the time they called us with permission to give the IV, he had definitely improved. They also told us at that time that a helicopter would be in to get him.

"A doctor from Churchill came in on an Allouette chopper. He examined Mr. Hauer and pretty much agreed with what we thought the injuries were. I remember that he also started a second IV. Then we got Mr. Hauer out of the wreckage and into the helicopter. It left right away for Churchill, but George and I stayed where we were. They didn't have room for two more so we just gathered up our gear and began to wait.

"By this time though, we had gone without anything to eat for several hours and we were getting pretty hungry. I remember that we were about to eat some of our own rations when we decided to see if there was any food in the plane." Howard laughs as he recalls the moment.

"There sure was food there — enough for a banquet — and us out on that godforsaken tundra with nothing around but mosquitoes. Anyway, we found some great Camembert cheese, lots of German sausage, and all these fancy little crackers and stuff — and we enjoyed it all! That was a meal I'll *never* forget."

After about two hours the helicopter returned for two stuffed SAR Techs. They rode in to Churchill where their own aircraft was waiting.

Subsequently, Hans Hauer was flown to Winnipeg, where, the next day, newspapers reported that although he had sustained a fractured spine and other injuries, his condition had been upgraded to "fair." A month later, Hauer's girlfriend wrote to the two SAR Techs, praised them, and thanked them for saving a life in the wilderness. Neither man heard from the pilot again.

Three weeks after the Hauer rescue, all SAR Techs in the Canadian Forces were given authority to administer intravenous therapy.

6

All in a Day's Work

Shortly before midnight on Saturday, March 30, 1975, one of the worst storms in history lashed the coast of British Columbia. Before the gale blew itself out some twenty hours later, several people were dead, scores were injured, and property damage was in the millions. As well, untold numbers were inconvenienced in a myriad of ways, through such things as hydro interruptions, ferry cancellations, washed out roads, and flooded basements.

At the height of the storm, winds were clocked at eighty to eighty-five miles per hour in several locations and the driving rain made travel of any kind virtually impossible. Throughout the lower mainland, from the coast to Kamloops, power lines were down, traffic lights were dark, and mature trees were twisted and torn from their roots. A heavy snowfall blanketed the Hope–Princeton highway.

In the Vancouver area, Stanley Park had to be closed, half a dozen ocean-going ferries dragged their anchors in English Bay, and fifteen light planes were either flipped over or badly damaged at the airport. Others would have been destroyed, had not their owners arrived to physically hold the machines down. A few were saved only because they were lashed to cars, trucks and steel fence posts embedded in concrete. A house under construction in Delta was flattened.

One of the large B.C. ferries, *Queen of Tsawwassen*, was tossed around during the gale and ended up with several gouges and dents in her hull, along with a bent propeller. The vessel had to be removed from service. At one point, all ferries between Vancouver and Vancouver Island were stopped, their cancellations resulting in hundreds of motorists lined up for boats that were not going to sail. Those in the vehicles spent hours in their cars, virtually marooned where they were. Fortunately, their plight was eased somewhat through the efforts of civil defence workers who brought them blankets and hot coffee.

Depending on the location, the storm was at its fiercest between 10:00 P.M. that Saturday and 2:00 A.M. the following day. In Victoria, the Armed Forces Rescue Co-ordination Centre received fifty-nine calls for help in those four hours alone. Most were from boaters in distress, who feared they were in danger of death, or at least imminent harm. In such cases, assistance was rendered as soon as conditions and available personnel permitted.

At Canadian Forces Base Comox, midway up the eastern coast of Vancouver Island and home of Search and Rescue Squadron 442, the first grey streaks of daylight were filtering over the mainland mountains as an Air Force Labrador helicopter was readied for work. Crew call-out had been at 5:10 A.M., and despite the high winds, the big chopper was in the air before 6:00. The pilots that morning were Captain Wilkinson and Major Carr-Hilton. In the back of the ship, the flight engineers were Master Corporals Kennedy and Meider. In 1975, only one Search and Rescue Technician was normally a part of the crew complement. On this day, it would be Master Corporal Bill Wacey, an Ottawa-born Para Rescue specialist who had come to the air force after three years in the army. He was 39 years old.

The Lab headed south, threading its way among the numerous islands that dot the Strait of Georgia. Just off tiny Ballenas, the anchored sailboat *Sly II* strained at her lines, both of which were being taxed beyond their capabilities. However, when Corporal Meider used a loud hailer to contact a couple who were on the yacht, they declined assistance, so the chopper moved on to Active Pass, a stretch of water between Galiano and Mayne Islands. "That was when our day *really* started," recalls Wacey. "We found four teenagers, two guys and two girls, all of them hanging onto a catamaran that was about to be smashed to smithereens against boulders along the shore. Those kids were wet, cold and scared."

Bill Wacey, former Para Rescue Technician, saved the lives of several people following a vicious storm in southern British Columbia in March, 1975.

The four had been in the wrong place at the wrong time. Several hours earlier, a coast guard hovercraft had been responding to a distress call, and because of the wild winds and rain, and the state of the sea at the time, it collided with the catamaran. The hovercraft was beached, and the young people had to fend for themselves.

"They were pretty happy to see us," Wacey says. "By the time we got there, they were pretty upset."

One of the flight engineers hooked himself into a safety harness and opened the door on the right side of the helicopter. The other cleared space in the back of the ship for passengers, while Wacey checked and rechecked his equipment, prior to going to the stricken vessel below them. He was already in a wetsuit.

"The winds must have been sixty or seventy miles an hour at that point," he says. "The chopper was bouncing all over the place, and the waves were really high. It was also raining."

Wacey was hooked onto the hoist cable and slowly winched down to the catamaran. The process took time, because the boat would rise to the top of a wave and then would immediately plunge into a trough. Often Wacey was almost on the deck only to be yanked into the sky when the boat dropped away under him. While all this was happening, the aircraft was being buffeted unmercifully as the pilots fought to remain in one place.

Finally, Wacey reached the boat and got a horsecollar rescue sling around one of the girls. He signalled to the hoist operator up above, and held on to the young woman as they were pulled to safety. Wacey then went back down — three more times — and got the others. On the final hoist however, he had trouble.

"I had just put the harness on the last guy," Wacey explains, "when the boat went out from under us. The two of us went down under the hull and the waves threw us against it. I was wearing a hard hat, so when my head banged against the boat, I was okay."

The young man was not so lucky.

"When he hit the hull, I heard a crack, and he broke his jaw, but I managed to hold on to him until the hoist operator got us up out of there. The boy was hurt and bleeding so we laid him down and worked on him until we got to hospital in Victoria. The poor kid was okay until I rescued him," says Wacey with a twinkle in his eye. "But he had a real sense of humour. On the way to the hospital he was trying to talk to me, and at one point said, 'My mother is going to be *mad* at you.' I asked him why and he tried to laugh when he said, 'Because you don't know how much she's spent on my teeth.' Several of them were loosened."

Even before the Lab reached the helipad at Victoria, the crew was informed of another problem near the ferry terminal at Tsawwassen. The teenagers were quickly turned over to the hospital emergency people, and within five minutes the chopper was back in the air.

"It was another sailboat," recalls Wacey, "this time maybe twenty-five to thirty feet long, with lots of cables, gear, and ropes all over the deck."

On board were two adults and two children, both youngsters under six years of age. The boat was sinking fast, and although it was not too far from the ferry terminal, people watching from there were powerless to assist. The seas were much too rough.

"We swung around over them," says Wacey, "but with all the gear on the deck down there, I knew I'd never be able to drop on it. I wondered then, and I still wonder today, why people don't toss stuff overboard when they're in real trouble. Making the boat lighter could keep them from sinking.

"Anyway, I talked things over with the engineers, and decided to have them put me in the water behind the boat and I would swim to it."

Corporal Kennedy hooked Wacey to the hoist, and he started down. The winds had slackened somewhat but the operation was far from easy. Just as the would-be rescuer touched the water, a swell pulled him under and dragged him, spitting and sputtering, away from the boat. Wacey got his bearings, then swung around and swam back towards it. As he grabbed a deck cable, another wave slammed him against the hull.

"Finally I was able to grab one of the kids," Wacey remembers, "but the little guy was so small, I was afraid he would flip out of the harness, so I just held onto him. We hoisted him over to the ferry dock and set him down. I told him to stay there and I would get his parents. He was crying through the whole thing."

On the dock itself, a spectator named John Garnham watched in awe as the operation took place. He would later describe the "hell of a courageous" helicopter crew for the March 31, 1975 *Vancouver Sun.*

"The chopper was having difficulty stabilizing itself about fifty feet above the boat," he said. "Finally they let a man down on a wire. He was swinging like a child on a swing and even fell into the water once. He harnessed up one of the kids and got him off, then the other. Then the chopper dropped the kids off on the causeway and went back for the parents."

"We got them all to safety," said Wacey, "but the boat was gone. Then we left."

In fact, a radio call directed Captain Wilkinson to pick up a very frightened woman from Saturna Island, midway between Vancouver and Victoria. "She had broken a leg trying to pull a sailboat in, but apart from that, was okay," says Wacey. "We dropped her off at the hospital in Victoria. She was also pretty worried about getting off the island, I guess," he adds. "She was hardly out of the helicopter when another call came in. This time we flew over to Mayne Island to pick up two girls."

This call would be even less pleasant than the ones that preceded it.

Two young women had been camping in a wooded area when the storm came up. At first, apparently, they felt it would pass and remained huddled in their tent as the rains swept over it. As the winds strengthened however, the tent was little protection for the two. A tall pine tree behind their shelter was ripped apart and it crashed onto the tent. The full weight of the trunk came down on 19-year-old Ottawa native Dierdre Jacques and crushed her skull. Her friend, Teresa Wojcihowicz, suffered serious back injuries in the incident.

"Both were in terrible shape when we got there," Bill Wacey explains. "The victim whose skull was crushed was unconscious, so I administered oxygen and used a syringe to help clear the blood out of her throat. The other woman was conscious at first and I looked after her as best I could."

Both the injured parties were placed in litters on the ground and hoisted into the chopper, which hovered just above the trees.

"They were alive when we got them into the helicopter," Wacey continues, "but I don't know to this day if either survived. I know I was awfully glad when we touched down at Vancouver General. I felt so bad for both of them. They never had a chance."

Several hours later, the hospital listed Teresa Wojcihowicz's condition as poor, but the injuries sustained by Dierdre Jacques had proven fatal.

"We got fuel sometime during the day," Wacey recalls, "and I grabbed a sandwich. I know I was still gulping it down when we got called again. A couple of boats had foundered just off Point Grey."

About 2:00 P.M., a nineteen-foot rented fishing boat carrying four males from Edmonton encountered choppy sea conditions at the mouth of the north arm of the Fraser River. As water sloshed into their craft, the occupants baled for their lives, but their efforts were in vain. The little vessel continued taking on water and within minutes slid beneath the waves. The four started swimming, but the cold, rough water was just too overpowering.

At about the same time, three people in an outboard who came to help ran into trouble. Their boat was tossed all over the place by the surf, and then it flipped upside down. Now seven souls were fighting for their lives.

By the time the big Lab appeared overhead, two men from the second boat had struggled up onto a beach, where they huddled together in a futile attempt to get warm. Wacey was lowered to them — twice — and each was hoisted into the helicopter.

"Both were suffering from exposure," he said. "I treated them on board the aircraft, and I was sure they would pull through. Then one of the engineers noticed another guy in a lifejacket floating in the water, so I went down again."

"It was a young boy, 13 or 14 I suppose. He was still alive, but was unconscious so I had a bit of a struggle getting him up. I started mouth-to-mouth as soon as we got him into the chopper, and I continued on the way to the hospital, but he was dead when we got there."

The helicopter returned to Point Grey and located one of the men from the first boat. Wacey was lowered to him.

"By this time, I had been in and out of the water so many times, I was exhausted. I knew he was pretty bad so I started mouth-to-mouth as soon as I got down to the guy. I kept doing so until I noticed that he had sand in his mouth and I realized I was giving mouth-to-mouth to a corpse. We turned him over to the Vancouver RCMP. When there was no sign of anyone else, we left."

But Bill Wacey's day was still not over. The man and woman on the *Sly II* who had refused help in the early morning now needed late-afternoon assistance.

"I think they tried to hold on as long as they could," Wacey says, with a touch of admiration in his tone, "but they finally found it impossible. When we got to them, they had only one line out, and they were on the top of the yacht, holding on for dear life. They also had their dog with them.

"I knew for sure they were coming up, and that the dog was as well when I saw the woman putting a coat on it, a scared little poodle.

"In the morning, I'd been reasonably sharp, but by the time of those last hoists, I was so tired I could hardly think, and I was careless. When hoisting from a boat where there are ropes and stuff on the deck, you always make sure none of them are around your feet or legs. As I was bringing the man up though, there was a cable around my foot and I didn't even notice. I was really lucky because I was able to shake it off partway up.

"Those folks were so pleasant, and they kept thanking me and the other guys. I really don't think they expected to survive. They were from Van Nuys, California. And even though we rarely hear from people we might have rescued, I did hear from them. We took them into Nanaimo."

It was dusk when the helicopter got back to Comox. The crew members disembarked and walked into the hangar. Wacey phoned his wife.

"I called Maureen to pick me up," he laughs, "but when she asked if I really needed a ride, I told her I guessed not. She had to have the car for something or other. I sure could have used a lift, but I didn't bother telling her I had had a hard day. I walked home alone. Later on, when she heard what I had gone through since early morning, she felt bad."

In his report of his day's activities, for which he was later awarded the Star of Courage for bravery, Bill Wacey wrote: "We conducted 12 double hoists, 11 were survivors, 1 was dead. There were three stretcher patients, 2 critical. We recovered 2 bodies and also recovered 2 people alive (no hoists involved). We searched and refuelled in between and took two Coast Guard members to hovercraft. We flew a total of 9.5 hours and I was in a wetsuit for 12 hours."

His conclusion was the ultimate in understatement: "Rather weary."

He didn't mention the poodle.

7

Fire at Sea

W hen the fire started, the ship was 170 miles out, in the frigid waters of the Gulf of Alaska. No rescue boats were nearby, and the weather was deteriorating. It was also late at night.

The Dutch luxury liner *Prinsendam*, with 510 souls on board, had left Vancouver three days earlier, en route to Yokohama, Shanghai, Hong Kong and Singapore. Most of the passengers were American, although there were some Swiss, a few Germans, and sixteen Canadians. Most were elderly. The cruise was scheduled for thirty days, with travellers shelling out up to $5,075 U.S. each for the fare.

Shortly before midnight on October 3, 1980, a small fire was reported in the vessel's engine room. Some smoke drifted through the ship, and to prevent panic, passengers were told that the fire had been minor, that it was under control, and that there was no cause for alarm. Most went back to bed, unconcerned.

The seven-year-old *Prinsendam*, with its Dutch officers and Indonesian crew, sailed on. The smoke dissipated, the alarm bells remained silent, and for a time, radio traffic from the ship became less frequent. But the lull did not last.

While all this was going on, a Canadian Search and Rescue Labrador helicopter under the command of Ken "Casey" Pettman was doing a medivac at Campbell River, halfway up the east coast of Vancouver Island. The co-pilot that night was Keith Gathercole.

"We had just picked up a guy who had crashed his car into a telephone pole," Gathercole remembers, "and we were airlifting him to hospital in Vancouver. As we flew down the Straits, I was listening to the HF radio, and I heard some conversation between a ship up in the Gulf of Alaska and an American Rescue Co-ordination Centre. The guy on the ship said they had an engine room fire, and then he gave his position. I grabbed a map, but when I realized the location was away off the edge of it, I knew the Americans would be looking after this one. After that, I more or less put the matter out of my mind."

The luxury liner *Prinsendam* burns in the Gulf of Alaska. The successful rescue operation that followed the fire involved, among others, Canadian Forces and United States Coast Guard personnel. (Photo courtesy Al Williams)

But the fire on the *Prinsendam* could not be controlled, and it gradually spread, despite the crew's best efforts to douse it. By 2:30 A.M. flames were licking at the carpet and anything else that would burn in the dining room. Smoke wafted through the hallways of the lower decks, and anyone in a cabin was ordered to assemble in a lounge on the main deck. In no time, the lounge too filled with smoke, necessitating a future demand that everyone move to the open air on the top deck. Because they were prevented from returning to their rooms, most of the passengers were still in their nightclothes.

In the meantime, Captain Cornelius Wabeke ordered his communications personnel to send out an SOS. The message was picked up by U.S. Coast Guard stations in Alaska, and several ships in the Gulf or close to it. One of these was the supertanker *Williamsburg*, out of Valdez, Alaska, bound for Texas with a load of crude oil. At the time of the SOS, the tanker was about one hundred miles from the *Prinsendam*.

The *Williamsburg* immediately sailed to the aid of the stricken liner. So did Coast Guard boats *Mellon*, *Boutwell* and *Woodrush*. By this time the United States Air Force base at Elmendorf, Alaska was involved, as was the RCC in Juneau. Soon the RCC in Victoria, British Columbia would be dealing with the matter as well; people there were already monitoring the situation.

Whether any of the passengers on the burning ship knew of the SOS is immaterial; they were much too occupied with personal concerns. And because they knew they would be cold once exposed to the chill of the night air on the top deck, some grabbed anything they could for warmth, from decorative tablecloths to lounge curtains. Once outside, many would later remember the shock of the cold, the brilliance of the ocean stars, and the confusion and uncertainty about what was going to happen next.

As the passengers milled about, waiting for direction, six members of a song-and-dance troupe from New York gathered in one corner and began singing. They did several Rodgers and

Hammerstein tunes, from "Oklahoma" to "The Sound of Music," and lifted the spirits of most. Some, however, were uncomfortable, feeling that the singing had all the overtones of the Titanic disaster.

Meanwhile, down below, the ship's firefighters were losing the battle. For that reason, the order that everyone feared finally came, in a the disembodied, sonorous announcement from the bridge: "Abandon ship!" Alarm bells rang incessantly, and in near-pandemonium lifeboats were readied and quickly filled, often by crew members who elbowed elderly passengers aside. In several instances, the Dutch officers had to order, and even physically remove, members of the ship's company who rushed to claim the first lifeboat spaces for themselves.

The *Prinsendam* carried six large lifeboats and two motorized tenders. The lifeboats could carry about sixty-five people, but in the confusion of loading, many more were jammed aboard a couple of them. Others had far fewer. None of the boats had much in the way of shelter, and some passengers would later claim that there was neither food nor water on board. All boats were off the ship and bobbing on the sea's surface by dawn. A small contingent of firefighters remained behind to fight the blaze, which continued to worsen. Some hours later, however, even the firefighters had to go. The *Prinsendam* was doomed.

Down in the lifeboats, some passengers thought their fate would be no better. They huddled together for warmth, but often without leadership or direction. As the hours passed, the little vessels drifted far across an increasingly choppy sea. Even the ship they had left drifted — by some estimates — as much a seventy-five miles in the hours after it was abandoned. Almost as soon as the lifeboats were launched, the winds rose, and heavy fog blanketed the sea. By now, the odds of this becoming a major maritime catastrophe were very high.

Yet, as quickly as the makings of a disaster grew, cries for assistance were heard.

For one thing, the *Williamsburg's* proximity to the burning *Prinsendam* would prove to be extremely fortunate. It took less than seven hours for the supertanker to close the gap between the two vessels, and once near the burning liner, the oil tanker was used in unexpected ways. For starters, it became an airport.

The supertanker *Williamsburg* became an impromptu airport and hospital during the rescue operations following the fire on board the luxury liner *Prinsendam*. (Photo courtesy Al Williams)

The ship was a thousand feet long, and fully loaded was as stable in the water as a boat could be. Its acres of deck space were flat and relatively uncluttered. Its size made it easy to see from the air, and its communication system was state of the art. In short, it was a place where a helicopter could land with relative ease.

Not long after the mayday signal, air-refuelable U.S. military helicopters were in the air and heading for the *Prinsendam*. So were two Canadian choppers and two Buffalo search planes from 442 Squadron in Comox, along with a big, lumbering Argus from 407 Squadron. The first Canadian helicopter to go was the one Casey Pettman and Keith Gathercole had been using for the Campbell River medivac.

"We were called in the early morning by RCC in Victoria," Gathercole said, "and they told us the Americans needed help.

When we left Comox, the place was really busy. There were all sorts of people coming in; the crews were flight planning, and the SAR Techs were loading what they thought they would need.

"On the way up, the weather between Comox and Port Hardy was terrible, so we could not go VFR [Visual Flight Rules], but had to fly IFR [Instrument Flight Rules] at six thousand feet or so. With the load we had on board, and the fuel we had on board, we didn't have a hope if we lost an engine, but because it was an emergency, we went. Later on, we came down much lower, switched to VFR, and skimmed the water at about a hundred feet. By then, we had unbelievable tail winds so we got to Sitka, Alaska in good time. We landed there with eleven people on board — the crew of six, plus five extra SAR Techs."

On the way into the Alaskan airport, the men in the back of the helicopter had noticed an unusual smell which they thought might be from the electrical system. But because no-one was able to identify the source, the aircraft was checked over carefully by the engineers once on the ground. No problems were found.

"We took off on max fuel," Gathercole recalls, "and then we headed out into the gulf to look for lifeboats. Our second helicopter was only a few minutes behind us.

"We were not much more than forty minutes out when we noticed our nav aids [navigational equipment] didn't seem to be working right. We were still trying to find out what was going on when they quit entirely. So here we are: no nav aids, half a mile visibility, and the whitecaps are a hundred feet below us. Then our troubles got worse.

"The guys in the back started yelling, and all of a sudden smoke began billowing up the left side of the airplane, beside me. There was a fire on board, but at first we couldn't figure out where it was. We knew it was electrical. Then somebody noticed that an electrical distribution box was red hot. But they didn't dare use a fire extinguisher on it in case of an explosion.

"I remember Casey saying, 'Get ready guys, we're going into

the water.' Then he reached up and turned our ELT on. In the meantime, we're out here in the middle of nowhere, in the fog. And the other planes in the area don't know where we are. We don't know where we are. We're a hazard to them. We're a hazard to ourselves.

"Gary Flath and John McLellan were up front in the helicopter behind us, and they called as soon as they heard our ELT. We told them we had no nav aids, that we had a fire in the back, and that we were probably going to ditch. They said they were coming to us, and that made us feel a lot better. In the meantime, we were putting on immersion suits while Casey was turning things on and off to see if anything he did made a difference. Then, when he turned off the number one generator, the smoke stopped!

"So instead of ditching we decided to wait a while and see what happened. The smoke eventually cleared up completely, but because we couldn't navigate, we were no good to anyone. Then our radios started acting up, and everyone out there knew we were in trouble. So when an American Herc that had been out there refueling their helicopters offered to lead us in to shore, we accepted.

"He took us to Yakutat [in Alaska], which by this time had become a passenger reception centre. Some of our SAR Techs stayed there to help the people from the *Prinsendam* as they were brought in. At least three others, who had come in from Comox on one of the Buffalos — Ron Holliston, Bob Mondeville and Chris Girden — flew out to the search area on an American Coast Guard helicopter. They landed on the oil tanker and assisted as the people from the lifeboats were taken there."

Meanwhile, out in the Gulf, those in the lifeboats were finding out firsthand how treacherous the area could be. Angry twenty-five-foot waves tossed the little boats around; cold, raw north winds added to the discomfort, and virtually everyone was seasick, half-frozen, terrified and unbelievably lonely. And when dense fog settled over the sea, feelings of being lost forever became too real for many. "We prayed for the safety of everyone," was the way Dora Brownhill of Chatham, Ontario described the ordeal to a *New York Times* reporter two days later. Sonna Criss and her husband William, from Toronto, who were celebrating their thirtieth wedding anniversary, would never forget the experience. "We were so cold," Mrs. Criss told the Associated Press on October 6, "I don't believe we could have survived a night in the boat. It was a nightmare. I don't know what else to call it."

As soon as Gary Flath realized the other Canadian chopper was on its way to safety, he and his crew continued on to the *Williamsburg*. They landed on the deck of the supertanker, dropped off half a dozen medical personnel, and then went out to look for lifeboats. In addition to the pilots, the crew on board consisted of flight engineers Frank Amadio and Randy Bourquin, and SAR Techs Bob Lang and Al Williams. Williams takes up the story: "When we got to our first lifeboat, I was hoisted down into it. Then I started putting one passenger after

SAR Tech Al Williams assisted in the saving of several lives following the *Prinsendam* fire in the Gulf of Alaska. (Canadian Forces photo)

another into the horsecollar and they were taken up into the Lab. At times, you would put the collar on somebody, the lifeboat would slide off a big wave, and the person would immediately be fifteen or twenty feet in the air.

"The first hoist I did was an injured crewman who had hurt himself when he jumped off the ship. I managed to get the collar about half onto him, then the boat dropped off a big wave and the guy fell into the ocean. I grabbed him, hauled him back in, and we did it again. All the other hoists were okay. Once we got going, we were hoisting one person a minute. When we had everyone, we flew to the oil tanker, dropped the people off, then went to find another lifeboat. Bob Lang went down into the second one, and I did the third.

"We were hoisting five or six people for every one the Americans took off. They did not put one of their own people down into the lifeboats, so there was no one there to take charge. They were doing two at a time by lowering a basket, but people were fighting to be hoisted first. That made it a lot slower.

A passenger from a lifeboat belonging to the burning ocean liner *Prinsendam* is hoisted into a Canadian Forces Labrador helicopter in the Gulf of Alaska. (Canadian Forces photo)

"When Bob or I were in the boats, we told the passengers the order they would go. When we were hoisting, I would get somebody in the collar, hang onto the line to the boat myself, then jump into the water. If I didn't, the *Prinsendam* crew who were in the lifeboat would trample all over everybody in order to get hoisted first. By hopping out of the boat, I kept them from grabbing the hoist, and there was some order. It kept people from rushing the hook and getting us nowhere. It also kept some of the elderly passengers from clinging to me in panic — but the biggest problem by far was the crewmen.

"I had to knock some of them back about three rows. I couldn't believe it. Most of the passengers were quite elderly, and many of the women were just in nightgowns. They had no way to defend themselves, or insist on their turn. But the crew — I had to hit some of those guys as hard as I could to keep them back.

"I wanted to get the old folks first, but some of them found it hard to do. They would say, 'I can't do this. I can't do this.' But if I couldn't coax them, I would grab them, put the collar on, and the next thing they knew, they were sitting safely in the back of the helicopter. In general, the passengers were not panicking or crying. They waited their turn — but they were sure upset at the crew. So was I."

In all, Flath and his men rescued forty people from the sea. After the first thirty-one were safely on board the *Williamsburg*, the Lab was tasked to look for a missing lifeboat that had not been sighted since it had been put overboard. They found the boat, in heavy fog, far from the main search area. And even though the Lab was almost out of gas, the men hoisted nine persons into the helicopter and then waited to direct an American Coast Guard cutter to the scene so the remaining passengers could be saved. Already at beyond bingo fuel (the point at which low-fuel warning lights come on), the Lab limped into Yakutat and barely reached the end of the runway. One engine flamed out as it taxied to the terminal. A minute or so later and the helicopter would probably have crashed into the sea. No-one dared tell the passengers this of course; they had already endured too much.

For his part, Bob Mondeville would look back on his time on board the *Williamsburg* as one of the most interesting episodes in his SAR Tech career. He, Holliston and Girden helped treat and take care of over 260 *Prinsendam* passengers, in confined quarters where a kitchen had become an infirmary. Once checked for hypothermia, shock, bruises and exhaustion, the patients were tucked away in every available nook and cranny on the ship — which, despite its great cargo-carrying capacity, housed about thirty crew — all of whom offered their personal quarters to the survivors.

Later, Mondeville described the various medical procedures he performed — from starting IVs to administering oral medication, to the catheterization of two male patients who were in agony because of renal failure. (He was later annoyed because mention of the latter procedure was deleted from the official report on the mission.) He and his mates sailed to shore on the *Williamsburg*.

In the end, the rescue of the entire passenger and crew complement of the *Prinsendam* was a remarkable feat. No lives were lost, but without the efforts, the daring, and the unselfish contribution of life-savers from two nations, many would certainly have perished.

As is often the case, the American participants in the operation were the recipients of medals, praise, and the thanks of a grateful nation. The Canadians who risked their lives to save so many received no medals, little praise, and only the thanks of an occasional passenger who took the time to express it.

The operation was covered in the Canadian papers, but often in a way both irritating and unfortunate. For example, one of our best newspapers, the *Vancouver Sun*, had writers on the scene who did praiseworthy reports describing the work of our air force participants. However, when it came to the final word about the rescue, the *Sun* praised the Americans alone. In the paper's editorial on October 7, 1980, the editors referred in general to the rescue operations, and then stated that "the U.S. Coast Guard emerge as heroes." No mention of our Canadian heroes at all.

And the once-beautiful blue-and-white *Prinsendam*? It sank.

Many of the survivors of the fire on board the *Prinsendam* came ashore at Sitka, Alaska. In all, over 500 people were plucked from the ocean in a remarkable rescue feat.
(Photo courtesy Al Williams)

8

The Fury of a Flood

The Sea to Sky Highway 99 runs from Vancouver, British Columbia to the village of Whistler, some seventy-five miles north. Today, Whistler is known as one of the finest ski resorts in the world, while the highway leading to it is generally wide, well marked, and pleasant to drive. But a few years ago, neither the road nor its destination were particularly praiseworthy.

In 1980, Whistler existed as a resort, but then it was much smaller, less known, and generally frequented by skiers who demanded more challenge than Grouse Mountain offered. Gourmet restaurants either didn't exist or were still anomalies in the wilderness. Most of the hotels had yet to be built, and some people still remember that the best ski trails once ended in the garbage dump.

That same year, the road from Vancouver was a challenge to drive, a highway that even the locals cursed. To outsiders, it was just damned scary. There were far too many tight turns, stretches without guardrails, frequent washouts, and no place to pass if you were unlucky enough to get stuck behind a logging truck. And then there were the unexpected obstacles: the rocks on the road, the deer in your headlights, the drivers who thought this was Daytona.

But years ago, as today, there was the weather.

When you left Vancouver, the sun was shining, the road was dry, and all was well with the world. By Horseshoe Bay, the sun had gone. At Britannia Beach, you noticed a few drops on the windshield. At Squamish, it was drizzle, and just before you reached the Garibaldi Highlands, the rain was torrential. But farther on, there would be fog, sleet, and likely snow. The powder at Whistler would be great, if you could only get there.

These were the thoughts of hundreds of people who planned on being in Whistler for Christmas in 1980. The weather had been warm over much of British Columbia, and in fact, on Boxing Day, the temperature was fifteen degrees Celsius in Vancouver, a record high for the date.

And there was the rain: heavy, relentless, and everywhere. So much of it that the snow at Whistler, and on all the surrounding mountains was melting. Water levels in the area lakes — Cheakamus, Daisy and Garibaldi — were much higher than usual, and the rivers that emptied them into Howe Sound, and ultimately the Pacific Ocean became roaring cauldrons that swept away all before them.

In the largest town north of Vancouver, Squamish, wary residents watched as the river of the same name rose and inundated their town, forcing the evacuation of a trailer park and other homes closest to the water's edge.

To the north, things were worse. The Cheakamus River, a normally rather innocuous mountain stream, was at flood height, and in its rampage to the sea had become extremely dangerous. In particular, it threatened several cottages between it and Highway 99. Some of the most vulnerable were partly surrounded by water even in dry seasons; now they were sitting in a vicious, moving maelstrom.

Martin Thompson works out of Nanaimo now, but in

December 1980, he was a 24-year-old constable at the Squamish Royal Canadian Mounted Police detachment. In the course of his duties, he had cause to patrol the area north of town, and he knew and was known by many. Among those were cottagers along the Cheakamus, who looked upon this genial, outgoing young Mountie as a friend. They were generally glad to see him, but never more so than when he arrived unexpectedly that Christmas evening. He had come to check on them because he feared that the flooding might pose a threat to their homes. His fears were realized.

The water was already lapping at the foundations of some of the houses, and would probably soon do the same to others. But one cottage in particular was surrounded by water, because a rickety little bridge leading to it had been torn away by the raging river. The family living there was trapped.

Thompson immediately called his office, described the situation as he saw it, and suggested that the dispatcher on duty ask the air force for help. A helicopter was needed — in a hurry.

"I remember being at home in Comox when I got a call from RCC in Victoria," Search and Rescue pilot Keith Gathercole said. "It was almost nine o'clock at night and they told me a fishing boat near White Rock was in trouble and we were being sent down there to see what we could do. That got changed later though, when one of our Buffalos responded. Instead, they

Keith Gathercole, left, and Gerry Gray risked their lives to save people trapped by rising flood waters near Squamish, British Columbia.

told us to go across to Squamish because two adults and two children were trapped in a house on the Cheakamus River."

"I was on standby at the time," former flight engineer Gerry Gray recalls, "and I had a feeling we likely would have to go out. It was a terrible night, high winds, heavy, heavy rain, and pitch dark. People never get lost or in trouble in nice weather, but when it's really bad, the phone rings. Sure enough, it rang."

Gathercole, Gray, and the rest of the crew — co-pilot John McLellan, SAR Techs Craig Seager and Steven Gledhill, and the second flight engineer, Dave McMaster — drove to the airport and took off, about an hour after being called.

"It was really rotten flying weather," Gathercole continues. "The wind was blowing the helicopter around a lot, and because of the heavy rain and low cloud, it was hard to see. There are quite a few lighthouses down through the Strait of Georgia, so we used these for navigating. The first was Sisters, off Comox, then there were others at Nanaimo and Vancouver. You had to know which one you were heading for though, because it was easy to get lost.

"When we got to Horseshoe Bay, you couldn't see a damned thing. We were quite low over the water and some of those islands are fairly high. The trees on the tops were far above us and it would have been easy to hit them. I finally decided the whole thing was hopeless, so I told the guys I was going into Vancouver to wait for a break in the weather.

"But on the way we met a Hughes 500 helicopter going the other way. He was carrying Emergency Measures people into Squamish and he told me on the radio that he was going to try it. I thought, hell, if he can do it, so can I. He was smaller and more manoeuvrable than we were and I decided I'd follow. So we turned around, and Christ, once we were back over Horseshoe Bay, you could see the lights of Squamish reflecting off the low cloud base. The rain storm had been up in Howe Sound, and had blown out, so we followed the highway all the way to Squamish. I remember thinking that at this rate, this thing is going to be easy. Foolish thought."

Gerry Gray describes the trip up Howe Sound: "We all had headsets on, and we were all listening on the radio. Nobody said much as we were going in, because you didn't want to break in when the pilot was talking to the tower or something. The trip was very slow and very cautious, and when we got to Squamish, we could see that half the town was under water.

"At first, we couldn't find the airport because the weather suddenly got worse. The airport is north of the town there, and once the lights were behind us, everything was dark."

"I had been there only once before," Keith Gathercole adds, "and I kept trying to remember what the area looked like, where the highest hills were, that sort of thing. We also were worried about power lines that had been strung across the valley. You could never see them at night. Anyway, instead of runway lights, we flew over some car lights, and dropped down to have a look. It turned out that they were police cars, forming a circle with their lights so we would know where to land."

Gathercole brought the big Labrador down, climbed out, and introduced himself to Martin Thompson. The police officer described the flooding problems to the north, and said that in his estimation, a family would die unless they could be helped. Gathercole nodded, and suggested that the Mountie come with them as a guide. He readily agreed.

"Martin briefed me," said Gathercole, "but as we stood there talking, it started to rain really hard. So we got into the helicopter and I taxied out. But as I did so, the rain was falling so bloody hard, the rotor blades were turning it into a fog. With the landing lights on, I couldn't see ten feet in front, so I turned them off, but it was no better. I figured if we tried to go anywhere in this, we'd all be dead, so I said, 'That's it, we're not doing anything until morning.'"

"The Mounties took us to a motel in Squamish," Gerry Gray explains. "They put us in a four-wheel-drive vehicle and away we went — and that drive scared the hell out of me. It was worse than flying blind in the chopper. We were just going to a *motel*, for God sakes, and there was no real hurry! But there is nothing more terrifying than a Mountie with a mission. Here we are, it's the middle of the night, and we're racing down this flooded road, on the crown because there's water on both sides, and we met a car going slowly and fairly cautiously. The cop doing the driving flipped on the roof lights and we went roaring past. It probably scared the other driver worse than the flood did. I know I was happy to reach the motel."

"It was probably one in the morning when we got to where they were taking us," Gathercole continues, "so I asked for a wake-up call because I thought that by 5:00 or 5:30 we might be able to see something and we would try it again. But when I tried to sleep, the adrenalin is pumping and I'm lying there, not able to sleep at all. And I kept thinking of those poor people trapped in the river, and my not being able to do anything to help.

"But about an hour later, I heard a car door slam and a couple of guys talking, and I knew the RCMP were back to get us. Sure enough, I opened the curtains and looked out, and that's who it was. They came up to my room and asked if there was anything at all we could do. Apparently an embankment up the valley was in danger of collapse and they were afraid a lot of people would be killed. So I got the guys up, told them about the situation now, and away we went. Martin came with us."

Gathercole decided to try to follow Highway 99 north. By now the weather had improved somewhat, but the clouds were black and low over the Cheakamus valley, and visibility was far from good.

"John McClelland was reading the map as we went along," Keith Gathercole says, "and the others were looking out both sides because it was black as hell. The floods had taken out the power, so there were no lights anywhere at all. I remember sensing where the bigger hills were; they were the blackest parts outside. We were not sure where the power lines were, so we went pretty slowly.

"We had been flying for a while when we saw a light, what looked like some kind of signal. I briefed the crew as we approached and turned on the lights, the landing lights and the search light when we got to about three hundred feet. The damned winds started whipping up again as we got down, and this didn't help much — nor did the trees around this cabin. The trees were all about 120 feet high and they were right up close to it. At that time we only had about 130 feet of usable cable on the hoist."

In the rear of the chopper, SAR Tech Steve Gledhill elected to go down. It was well known by all the military people on board that if Gledhill couldn't effect a rescue on this wild night, no one could. He was 30 years old, over six feet tall, and as good at his trade as any SAR Tech before or since. Modest to a fault, he did his job, and did it well, without ever boasting of his prowess.

As Gledhill was lowered on the steel cable from the helicopter, wind gusts swung the SAR Tech in an arc above the trees, and the winter rain streamed down his face. Gary Gray paid out the cable, and as he did so, noted with some alarm that the wild swings were becoming worse. His fears were justified.

Just at the point where Gledhill was slightly below the house roof, the wind took him, slammed him against the front of the building, and before he could either brace himself or prevent it, caused his feet to crash through an upper window. He was then thrown sprawling onto the rain-slick roof. Desperately, he clutched at the sodden shingles, and frantically tried to regain his balance.

But to no avail.

He slithered down the roof, flailing hopelessly around, doing all he could to keep from being tossed into the water that boiled about the building. Then, just as he lurched over the eve, the hoist cable snapped taut and jerked him into the air like a weight on a rope.

"I felt Steve hit," Gerry Gray explains. "And he told us afterwards that there was no grip on the wet cedar shakes, so he lost his balance and went zipping down the roof. There were hydro lines leading away from the house and he was sure he'd hit them. But when he ran out of cable, he came to a grinding halt. At that point, I thought I'd better get him up out of there."

But even though he could easily have just been killed, Steve Gledhill demanded to be lowered again. There were people down there who had to be helped, and he firmly intended to do what he could for them. After a hastily revised set of flashlight signals between himself and Gray, the SAR Tech swung out into the storm.

This time, he received a shock of a different order when he got to the house. Instead of the four people the rescuers had come for, only two were there — a man and a woman. It was only after meeting them that Gledhill, and later the crew up above, learned that this was not the family that Martin Thompson had called about several hours before. In any event, Steve Gledhill went about saving the lives of the two and the helicopter flew on.

"Those folks were really stuck," pilot Gathercole says. "And if they had not signalled, we would have never even known about them. They couldn't get out, and in all probability they would have died there. Thank God we saw their light — and all it was a candle. The power was off, of course.

"So now, we still haven't found the people we wanted, but Martin said he knew the river, and if we just followed it along, he would point out the cabin when we came to it. But because of the flooding, the river was ten times its normal width; it wasn't in its normal course, and it was totally different.

"I can remember Martin looking down at what looked like a goddamned lake, and saying 'Holy shit, I don't know *where* I am.' The water had risen so much during the night. But around about that time Craig Seager thought he saw something at a river bend. We had actually passed over the spot, but when he yelled, we turned around and went back. It turned out that this was the family we'd come for in the first place."

Craig Seager went down.

All around him were towering trees, swaying in the wind, and the cable to which he was attached would only allow him to go so far. He could not get down to the cabin below in a direct line, so he decided to let Gray drop him into the raging river in front of the building, and from there he would wade the rest of the way. Unfortunately however, as soon as he got into the water, the ferocious current swept his feet from under him and he disappeared below the surface.

"I had no idea what happened," says Gerry Gray. "It was so dark, and the search lights weren't much help. I was waiting for him to signal that he was down, but he never did, and then the cable got tight. I figured something was wrong, so I pulled him up again. The second time he got down okay."

Seager reached the house and found two adults and two children, including a 3-year-old boy and a small baby. He took up the mother and baby together, his first-ever triple hoist. Then he went back for the older child. This time, he had trouble.

The boy would not come.

Seager pleaded with the child, cajoled, got the father to help, but to no avail. The little guy had no intention of going with this strange man, up into the sky, in a storm, in the middle of the night. Finally, in exasperation, the SAR Tech grabbed the boy, put the rescue horsecollar around him, and went to signal to the chopper to be lifted.

But the collar slipped off over the youngster's head; the device was really meant for an adult.

On the second try, Seager grabbed the terrified little boy with one arm, held the cable with the other, and signalled Gerry Gray to haul away.

The first few feet were okay.

Then the child started to scream, flailing around with a strength well beyond his years. He pounded Seager across the face and neck and kicked ferociously at the SAR Tech's groin.

Seager held the little bundle of fury closer to ward off the fists, but the testicle-kicking was not as easy to prevent — or ignore. The trip up seemed to be without end. Five feet from the chopper door, and not much farther beneath the screaming propellers overhead, the boy increased his protests. Had it not been for the strong arms of flight engineer Dave McMaster, he might have broken from Seager's grasp and fallen to his death below. McMaster hustled the child through the plane to his waiting mother.

One hoist to go — this time Steve Gledhill.

But there were more problems.

When the SAR Tech was about eighty feet out into the night, the cable to which he was attached began to swing in a wide circle in the fierce winds. The arc became more and more pronounced, and nothing either Gray nor Gledhill did could stop it. Gathercole reversed the helicopter, but because they were in what amounted to a clearing in the bush, had almost no room to maneuver. Gledhill swung, like a weight on the end of a rope, and without warning, hit the top of a pine tree and spun around it. The cable came tight, and the SAR Tech was trapped. He ended up clinging to the tree with the rope wound around the trunk above him. Now, the helicopter was tied to the tree.

Luckily, Gathercole was able to keep the machine steady until both he and Gray worked a way out of the dilemma.

"Gerry Gray was the consummate professional in the whole thing," Gathercole recalls. "He was so calm about it. Because I couldn't see down to Steve, Gerry directed me back and forth, sidewise and back until we actually unwound the cable.

"He'd say, 'Okay, move it back two feet, now right a foot, now ahead two feet,' and so on. I had a big pine tree brushing the window for reference and the unwinding seemed to take a long time. All the while, the poor SAR Tech is still down there holding onto the tree."

Finally, Gledhill was free and Gray lowered him to the ground. Two minutes later, he signalled to be brought up — alone. The man refused to come.

"We couldn't believe it," Gathercole explained. "The guy's standing in water; we can see his house washing away, and there are big fir trees, roots and all floating downstream. As we watched, parts of the house fell down.

"Meanwhile, we're running out of gas."

Everyone knew the man in the river would be dead in minutes unless he was rescued. Gledhill turned to the man's wife for advice. She and Martin Thompson had a hurried conference.

"Just go down and *make* him come!" the woman ordered. "Don't give him a choice!"

Gledhill grabbed the hoist.

Up front, the fuel warning lights came on.

As soon as he touched down, Gledhill simply told the man he was coming, wrapped the collar around him, and Gray hoisted both. In the meantime, Gledhill and co-pilot John McClelland prepared for an emergency landing.

"All this time, I'm looking around trying to figure out where I could put down," Gathercole explains. "I thought we'd never get back to town; there just wasn't enough gas. But John was calculating our fuel situation, looking at a map, and trying to decide if we could make it. Then I looked at him; he looked at me and we made the decision to try.

"Luckily, it was almost dawn, so we could more or less see where we were going. Thank God, we made it — just."

The long night was over.

9

For Better or for Worse

In August, 1981, three friends from Channel 11, a television station in Hamilton, Ontario, went on a canoe trip into the Northwest Territories. Their goal was to paddle a series of interconnecting waterways to Yathkyed Lake, an 860-square-mile body of water a thousand miles north of Winnipeg.

The trio — Hank Pasila and twins Reg and Dan McGuire — had planned their trip with precision. After all, they had talked about it for over ten years, beginning when a friend named Rod Johnston had offered to pick them up when their journey was over. He would do so in his own plane.

"My offer was just a spontaneous thing," Johnston admits today. "We were all working at the station at the time, and they used to talk about making this canoe trip. I didn't even have a pilot's licence then, let alone a plane — but I hoped to get both later on."

And he did.

Winnipeg-born, Johnston spent most of his youth in Lynn Lake, the northern Manitoba town founded by Sherritt

Gordon Mines, where his father worked. The family moved there in 1952.

As a youngster in such surroundings, Johnston became enamoured with flying, and the romance and excitement it entailed. He could tell you if it was a Beaver or a Norseman overhead, who owned the machine, and the name of the pilot. He knew as well that if the motor on a Norseman was cut suddenly, it backfired. Three backfires from a circling aircraft meant that the pilot needed a cab after landing, so a local taxi would be dispatched. And when he was not watching planes overhead, Johnston was gassing them, cleaning windscreens, and running errands for the owners.

He also knew of planes that crashed, and the searches for them.

Following their safe arrival at Lynn Lake, Manitoba, survivors of a plane accident pose with the men who parachuted to their aid. They are, from left: Hank Pasila, SAR Techs Larry Scott and Arnie Macauley, Reg McGuire, Rod Johnston, and Dan McGuire.
(Photo courtesy Rod Johnston)

Years later, long after he became disenchanted with the radio and television world where he once envisioned a career, Johnston returned to Lynn Lake, but by now he had become a dentist. He practiced locally, but drew on his love of flying to attend to patients in remote areas, sometimes a hundred miles from home. Once a month, he and one or two of his staff would pack his dental equipment into his Cessna 185, and they would fly to a village where, by working long hours, and often almost nonstop, they could compress a week's work into two or three days. He did this for six years and loved it. In the course of time, he met and married his wife Lynn, a budding cartoonist. (Appropriately enough, he met her at an airport.) By 1981, they had a son and a daughter.

Meanwhile, the three adventurers back at Channel 11 were still planning their trip. At long last, they contacted Rod Johnston about being picked up at the end of it. He was happy to oblige.

They started their journey at a placed called Ennadai, on a lake with the same name, and in the days that followed went down it and into the Kazan, perhaps the most popular river for canoeists in the north. From there, they would go to Yathkyed Lake and the little round bay where Johnston would meet them. Pickup date was scheduled for Sunday, August 9, 1981. None of the trio had ever been to the Barrenlands before.

"It is about 425 miles from Lynn Lake to Yathkyed Lake," Johnston explains, "and because my Cessna did not have that much range, I filled extra gas cans and took them with me. But that summer, we had had a lot of forest fires, and their smoke became a problem as I got farther north. By the time I got to where I was supposed to meet the guys, I was essentially on instruments, and I couldn't see a thing. I decided it would be crazy to risk a landing, so I had to turn around and fly home. The next day was clearer, so I went back.

"Before I left, I told Lynn, my dad, the Flight Service people at the airport, and one or two others exactly where I was going. I filed a flight plan, and my plane had an ELT. It was fairly windy on the way up, and it was overcast, but the smoke was no longer a problem."

Even though Johnston was a day late reaching his friends, the canoeists were not alarmed. They got to the arranged spot and, to combat boredom as much as anything else, roamed around picking up little sticks for firewood. They looked a bit more grizzled than usual, but were content because their trip had been a success. The area was essentially treeless, a flat, rocky land that stretched forever. It only grudgingly tolerated incursions from afar.

Johnston circled out over the lake, turned into the wind and set the float plane down. The time was about 11:00 A.M. He had made good time, particularly so because there had been one fuel stop along the way. The greeting he received was effusive, but he was not sure whether it was in spite or because of the fact that he was late.

"The wind off the shore was pretty strong, as I recall," Johnston says, "and the rocks on the edge of the lake were perhaps eight inches in diameter. The floats were bumping into them, as I lowered the wheels to hold the plane in place because there was no place to tie up. There was no beach or anything like that.

"I remember climbing out, and like a typical bush pilot, I wasn't dressed very well. I had just a jean jacket on, and I was cold right away. Somebody gave me a lifejacket, and I put it on for warmth. I was wearing Kodiak boots, but the others all had rubber boots."

The four men loaded the plane, stowing their gear behind the seats. Because the aircraft was a four-seater, space on board was at a premium. For this reason, only the canoe paddles were loaded. The canoe itself, along with the empty gas cans, were left behind for a later pickup by a charter outfit. Finally, when all the storage space on the Cessna was filled, Rod Johnston climbed into the left seat, and his passengers pushed the airplane away from shore. Then, to avoid getting wet, they hopped onto the right pontoon. The motor was not running.

By this time, it was quite windy, and the waves on the lake were a couple of feet high. The strong northeast wind tugged at the left wing, raising it higher and higher as the aircraft blew away from the shore. Meanwhile, one after the other, the men climbed off the pontoon and squeezed inside. As each did so, the right float dipped a bit lower into the water. But then, just as Rod

Johnston started to turn the propellor, three unfortunate factors came together at once. An unexpected, strong gust of wind caught and lifted the left wing, the last man to board heaved himself off the pontoon where he had been standing, and the right wingtip dug into a lake wave. In an incredible instance of bad timing, the little aircraft rolled to the right, hesitated slightly, and flipped over, upside down in the water like a turtle on its back. The last man in had no time to close the door.

"I remember seeing the left wing come up, and yelling, 'We're going to go over,'" Johnston explains. "Then we were upside down in the water, and everything was confused. I had read somewhere that in such a situation, the water pressure would prevent the doors from opening, but in our case, the right door had never been closed. Then I heard the crackling of our radios as they shorted out. I recall standing on what would have been the bottom of the left wing, then getting up to the surface. The other guys were already there.

"I felt terrible about what had just happened," he continues, "and the first thing I said was, 'Sorry about that, guys.' The fact that we were suddenly in a lot of trouble hadn't set in. My first reaction was simply one of embarrassment; my friends all laughed when I said I was sorry."

The bedraggled quartet sat on the inverted pontoons of the plane; the only part of the machine not below the waves. No-one was initially too concerned about their plight; no-one doubted that they would just drift to shore, and once there, would set up camp and wait for rescue. Unfortunately, such initial speculation was wide of the mark.

"We sat there for a long time," Johnston explains, "while we waited for the plane to drift with the wind across the lake to the opposite shore. That would have been three-quarters of a mile or so away. The temperature was about ten degrees Celsius, but because we were all soaking wet, and exposed to the strong wind, we got cold pretty quickly. I was the only one wearing a lifejacket, and as well, the only one wearing boots. The others had lost theirs getting out after we flipped. We tried diving down into the cabin for them, but because everything was packed so tightly, and with the water pressure, we could get nothing out. In the meantime, we were getting damned cold. I remember that after a while, we all started to shake.

"We were in the early stages of hypothermia, and after some discussion, decided we had to do something pretty soon. The plane did not seem to be going anywhere, and it was only later that we realized the top of the tail was anchored on the bottom, and instead of drifting, was only moving from side to side. The fact that we seemed to move, with respect to a couple of little bushes on the shore, actually fooled us. It was only the illusion of drifting. The lake where we were would have been about fourteen feet deep, because the top of the tail was fifteen feet high. We were about a thousand feet from shore."

By this time, the wind had increased in strength and the waves in height, and the distance to shore looked more and more forbidding. The overcast sky seemed to blend with the cold, gray, choppy water about them, and the view in any direction was dismal. It had also started to rain.

It was generally acknowledged by all four men that Hank Pasila was the most athletic of the group. In addition to being a fine canoeist, he was a marathon runner, and a strong swimmer. He would attempt to swim to shore and get the canoe, and with it rescue his friends. Johnston took off the lifejacket he was wearing, and Pasila put it on and slipped into the water. He was swamped immediately.

"I remember watching him fighting the waves," says Rod Johnston. "He would be visible one second, but then he would disappear. Then he would come up again. It took him a long time — and he was in shape. None of the rest of us could have made it. I told the others that Hank was our only hope. If he didn't make it, we were done."

The dire prediction almost came true.

Pasila struggled desperately, fully aware that he *had* to reach land. After what seemed an interminable time, he touched bottom, staggered up onto the rocks on the shore, and collapsed unconscious.

"We saw him lying there for the longest time," Johnston explains. "Eventually, he came around, didn't get up, but he dragged himself farther up on shore, and then literally crawled over to the canoe. This took a long time because it was about two hundred yards."

Once he reached the canoe, Pasila moved as if in a stupor. His actions were slow, laboured, the desperate motions of a desperate man. One by one, he picked up the empty gas cans and got them into the big canoe. Then, as the freezing trio atop the pontoons watched, Pasila somehow found a kind of superhuman strength, wrestled the boat off the rocks, and more or less fell into it. Luckily, it remained upright in the water, because it was no sooner floating than Pasila had passed out on its floor.

Then, in the most amazing development imaginable, the canoe started to drift, sidewise, away from the shore, and several minutes later bumped up against the upturned pontoons of the submerged plane. Carefully, the three men waiting there climbed aboard.

"By this time, Hank was not in very good shape," recalls Rod Johnston, as the memory of the incident flashes across his face. "His eyes were rolled back; all we could see were the whites and he was showing no sign whatsoever of coming around. Two of the guys knelt down in the canoe, and then lay flat on top of Hank, attempting to revive him with their body heat. The trouble was, we were all hypothermic, shivering and shaking, and Hank didn't seem to respond.

"The boat continued to drift, and eventually got to the opposite shore. None of us were in very good shape, but we managed to get out and pull the canoe out of the water. Hank was still out, and we were pretty worried about him."

Fortunately for the group, all had rudimentary understanding of how to combat the advanced hypothermia they were suffering.

"Our clothes were all soaked of course, and because they were, we were losing a lot of body heat," Johnston continues. "At first we took off Hank's clothes, then our own, and almost immediately we felt warmer. I remember shaking violently with my clothes on, but with them off, it was a lot better. At first we left our shorts on and we were still pretty cold, but when we had everything off, it was warmer. Amazing.

"By this time, the drizzle wasn't very pleasant, but we found some bushes and hung our clothes up to dry. After they'd blown in the wind for a while, they actually did dry. We were never warm enough, but the dry clothes helped.

"We had some matches in a waterproof tin, and luckily, when he went for the canoe, Hank threw the little sticks the guys had been collecting into it. He had put the gas cans in in case we had to have makeshift lifejackets if we'd fallen out of the canoe. They would have floated and we could have hung on to them.

"But our next problem was right then, we were all shaking so violently, we could not get the waterproof tin open to get a match. Each of us tried it, one of us would hold it and another would try. And we tried and tried and tried. We knew we had to have heat somehow. But then we found something we had not realized we had. In the pocket of the lifejacket — our one lifejacket — we found a Bic lighter. If one of us held it as steady as we could somebody else would rub his hand against the little wheel, and we thought maybe we could light it.

"We dragged the canoe around for a windbreak, and then made a little pile of sticks. We figured there might be a few drops of AV gas in the gas cans, and there was. We sprinkled it on the sticks, brought the Bic lighter in position, and got it going! The sticks started to burn, and by God, we had a fire! Things got a lot better then because Hank came around not long after that.

"Then we huddled behind the canoe, and waited to be rescued. I told the guys that everyone back home knew where we were, and that Lynn was pretty organized and she would get something going. I knew when we were overdue, a search would be started. But even though we watched the sky for the rest of the day, nothing happened. At that stage, I never thought about the ELT in the plane. Because we turned over the way we did, there was no real shock to the ELT and it had not gone off. Then when we sank I forgot to turn it on manually. So, no ELT."

*   *   *   *   *

In the meantime, at Lynn Lake, Manitoba, Lynn Johnston was completely oblivious to the events up on the Barrens. Her day had been full, and the endless deadline of her "For Better or For Worse" comic strip never eased. Household chores, as well as the needs of the children, Aaron, then 8, and Kate, 3, also kept her extremely busy. Soon, however, her daily routine would be totally shattered.

"We lived close to the airport at Lynn Lake," she told the author, "and you could easily walk down to it. And Rod was always on time, or just a little ahead of when he was expected. So I had no fear, and we were young, and Rod was always flying into these little places, so I never worried at all. But when he did not come back right on time, I took the kids and we decided we would walk to the airport and greet him. I remember that I had dinner ready for the guys.

"At first I wasn't too concerned, but when we got to the airport, I noticed that the Flight Services people looked worried. They knew Rod's habits, and they mentioned that he had never been that late before. They told me though, that they could not initiate a search until he was at least two hours over his ETA [Estimated Time of Arrival]. After some more time passed, and no plane, I began to get pretty concerned. I wasn't frantic because I don't get frantic, but I was certainly worried. But I knew that if his plane went down, there would be an effort to find him.

"Both of us knew about flying in the north, and we'd had some close calls, and we knew one of us could die up there. My first feeling was that if something had indeed happened, I had to collect my thoughts right away because I had two children I was responsible for.

"The people at the airport were wonderful. They told me that as soon as they knew anything, they would let me know right away. I took the kids and we went to Rod's parents' place. They lived even closer to the airport than we did. I broke the news to them, and to his brother who was there, and we talked about how we as a family were going to handle this — if it was a tragedy."

By this time, a call had gone to Search and Rescue in Edmonton, and a Hercules transport plane took off.

"Arnie Macauley and I were the SAR Techs on board," says Larry Scott, "but we didn't have much information at first. We just heard that a plane was overdue, that there could either be one or four guys on board. We flew to Lynn Lake and had another briefing there, and learned that an ELT hit had been picked up somewhere to the north, but that it wasn't clear where."

Lynn Johnston, creator of the popular comic strip "For Better Or For Worse", greets her husband Rod on his arrival home after he and three of his friends were rescued following an aircraft accident in the Northwest Territories. (Photo courtesy Rod Johnston)

Rod Johnston would later describe what had happened: "As I was flying up that morning, I talked to a man named Jack Austin who was flying a Beaver for an exploration outfit. At the time, I told him I was going to fly around some rain showers and I did. Shortly after this, he heard an ELT go off at about two in the afternoon, and thought it was me. He went to look for me, but didn't find me, and then the ELT stopped. Later on, when I did not come back on time, he was convinced it was me. So were the Search and Rescue guys.

"The ELT kept coming on every so often, and the Herc picked it up that evening. It turned out to be from a geological crew helicopter that had had a hard landing. The pilot was not aware of the fact that it had been activated, and by the time the air force searchers located the problem, all the people from the geological crew were in bed. They were in a number of tents, and the helicopter was parked nearby.

"The Herc flew over top, saw the tents and the chopper and thought they had found us. The message was radioed back to Lynn Lake. The Herc people couldn't get any response on the ground though, so they dropped a flare over the place. In no time apparently, people came running from the tents, wondering what in the hell was happening. Some of them thought the flare was a nuclear bomb, and it scared them a lot. Anyway, somebody in the Herc got the chopper pilot on the radio and told him to turn off his ELT."

"By this time, my mother-in-law was at home with me," Lynn Johnston explains, "and I got the call saying that Rod and the others had been found. But when the man mentioned several tents and a helicopter, I thought to myself, this cannot be. Part of me was rejoicing, and part was saying, this is not right, there is no helicopter.

"So I left the kids with Rod's mom and drove to the airport. There were several men in uniform there, and when they mentioned the helicopter again, I told them that could not be Rod.

"I said there *could* be no helicopter, and if there were any tents, there could only be two at most, not the five or six they had seen."

Not long after this, the Hercules returned to Lynn Lake, and the men on it promised to resume the search the next day — at first light. Several of them spoke to Lynn Johnston, and did their best to calm her fears. She remembers: "There were a number of air force gentlemen there in uniform, and what really struck me was how well they handled me. I was a potentially grieving widow, and I wanted for all the world for Rod to be found, but I had to tell them the people with the tents and helicopter were not the right ones. They believed me, and showed real concern for what I was going through.

"They handled me so well, with such tenderness and understanding, with compassion, yet not alarm. They told me what they were going to do first thing in the morning, how they were going to do it, where they would go, and so on. They told me I could come up to the airport and be a part of it, that I could phone them at any time. They treated me so well, I have to say I will never forget how confident I felt — even though I knew they might find a wreck with nobody alive in it.

"So the next morning, what they needed were spotters to look for Rod and the guys. They got the people at the airport to organize about ten spotters, and I asked if I could go. They told me, 'We understand that you want to go, but we'll let you go another time. We need you here. We may need information from you here.' They didn't actually come right out and say, 'We don't want you to find your husband's body,' but they never once made me feel as if I was in the way, or anything like that."

During these discussions at the airport, the four men at Yathkyed Lake huddled around their little fire, tried to keep warm, and slept, in twos, as best they could.

"Reg and Dan got the fire going nicely," says Rod Johnston, "but they kept it small so as not to burn all our wood. Then two of us would sleep, wrapped around each other for warmth. But in trying to sleep under these conditions, you got incredibly stiff. We didn't have a lot of clothes, but by nightfall, what we had was dry. While two of us slept, the other two kept the fire going. They also heated rocks to put around whomever was sleeping. After trying to sleep that way for a while, you would be in so much pain, you didn't mind changing places. We tried to keep up our spirits by calling 'room service' when we wanted another hot rock at our back. At one point, one of the guys looked at the other fellow he was lying beside and said, 'You know, you're the ugliest broad I've *ever* slept with.' We were not sorry when morning came."

Lynn Johnston's comic strip as it appeared some time after her husband Rod Johnston and his friends were rescued by Air Force SAR Techs following a plane accident in the Canadian north. (For Better Or For Worse © 1986 Lynn Johnston Prod. Inc. Reprinted with permission of Universal Press Syndicate. All rights reserved.)

It was early when the Hercules search plane flew north from Lynn Lake. And even though the searchers had been supplied with information from Rod Johnston's father as to where his son might be located, it was almost dark when the men were found.

And as it turned out, it was the upturned floats, and not the men, that were discovered first. When Larry Scott sighted the floats, both he and Macauley were sure they would find four corpses in the Cessna below.

The Herc made three or four passes over the floats as all eyes strained to see if somebody might have lived. On one of these flyovers, the searchers saw three men standing on a far shore.

"When we found those pontoons, we expected the worst for sure," Larry Scott recalls. "Then, when we saw the guys down there waving, it was probably the best sight in the whole world. It was getting close to dark, and Arnie and I decided we would jump to them after our equipment was down. Thank God, they were okay when we got there, although they had had nothing to eat for two days, and had been bitten by eight million bugs." During the day, the wind had eased, and millions of bugs became a constant irritant in the little camp on the lake shore.

Lynn and Rod Johnston today

"I'll never forget the looks on their faces when we got there," continues Scott. They couldn't stop smiling, and they didn't take long to dig into the rations we had. I remember being so happy for Rod Johnston. The poor guy had taken the whole thing so hard and kept blaming himself for the accident. It wasn't his fault at all. It was just one of those things. There was nothing he or anyone else could have done about it.

"Anyway, once we got them fed, and talking and laughing, we set up our tent, got some heat in it, and had a bit of a party there in the middle of nowhere. The Herc went back to the airport. The next day an Otter came in for us, and when we landed at Lynn Lake, half the town was waiting to greet us. Rod and Lynn Johnston were so well liked there, and everyone was glad there was a happy ending."

Shortly afterwards, another ELT went off, and the Hercules left for another search; fortunately, it ended the same way.

10

Heartbreak and Heroism

As pilot Mike Ruwald waited for takeoff clearance from the Edmonton control tower, he and his three passengers were looking forward to their trip to Vancouver. It was now April 1, and even though the calendar told them winter was over, it was still only three degrees Celsius in the Alberta capital. The day was cloudy, and according to weather reports it would also be cloudy at their destination, but Vancouver was several degrees warmer. There, at least, it would really be spring!

With the 30-year-old Ruwald that Friday in 1983 was his wife Bonnie Boucher, and their friends Deborah and Luke Reiche. Mike and Bonnie lived in nearby St. Albert, while the Reiches resided in Edmonton. All were originally from Ontario.

The plane they were travelling in was a four-seat Piper Comanche that Ruwald had rented in Edmonton that afternoon. The little single-engine aircraft was versatile, reliable and comfortable. It was also equipped with an Emergency Locator Transmitter.

The staccato sound of the controller's voice crackled in Ruwald's headset. He acknowledged the transmission, made a quick visual sweep of the instruments before him, and eased onto the runway. A minute or so later, the wheels of the plane left the ground. There were a few bumps as the plane climbed, but none of any consequence. Still at full power, the noise of the engine was constant, and the four passengers were buckled in and secure. The city gradually fell behind.

Ruwald's flight plan took them west by southwest over relatively level prairie, all of it still frozen, and dotted here and there with ice-covered sloughs, scrubby clumps of wind-blown pine and, at first, the nodding, ostrich-like movements of oil well pumps. Off to the right, the Yellowhead Highway ran west, past Wabamun Lake, Edson, and Hinton and on into Jasper National Park and the magnificent peaks of the Rocky Mountains. To the left, the Calgary Trail stretched to the southern horizon.

The minutes sped by, like the land below. In no time, it seemed, the Comanche was climbing above the foothills of the Rockies, and soon was high enough to clear the mountains themselves. Here, on a clear day, the scenery is spectacular, as beautiful as any on earth. But the very elements that make it so magnificent also make it treacherous to fly over, particularly in a small plane, for which the ceiling is low. For most of the trek over the rocks, the Comanche was in cloud, its pilot forced to use IFR. Yet Mike Ruwald was an experienced pilot, and his passengers trusted him implicitly. Soon they would be beyond the mountains, out of the clouds, and on the tarmac at Vancouver.

But this was not to be.

At first all went well at the higher elevation. The drone of the motor continued, the altimeter indicated adequate clearance over the topmost peaks, and the clouds that enveloped the plane made for a sense of security. It was like flying in cotton batting. If it had not been for the occasional air current updraught, movement of any kind would have been hard to measure. Progress was good.

Soon they were beyond the Great Divide, past the Monashee Mountains, and well above the Cascade Range that runs north-south, paralleling the Trans-Canada Highway between Hope and Lytton, B.C. Somewhere over that vast stretch of wilderness, Ruwald sensed a slight hesitation in the engine. He checked the gauges in front of him, but all appeared to be okay, and the hesitation stopped.

But then it returned, more pronounced, this time noticed by everyone.

Ruwald did more checks, reassured his passengers and kept his concerns to himself. But he also flipped the carb heat switch because he felt that an ice buildup in the carburetor might be the trouble.

For a time, all was well.

Then the hesitation returned, and the engine seemed to be losing power. Now all four adults in the little Comanche were worrying. Ruwald called the airport at Abbotsford, ahead and to the south of his position. He described the problems he was having, but said he was working to correct them. He also reported his position.

As he terminated his transmission, he noticed to his dismay that in losing power he had also lost height.

Now they were in the Lillooet Range of mountains, and he could not afford to fly lower. Yet the concern continued. The engine seemed to almost quit, roared into life, and quickly sputtered as badly as before. Then Ruwald signalled mayday and the motor stopped. The Comanche was at 5,300 feet when it slammed into the side of Chehalis Mountain.

*   *   *   *   *

"I was a SAR Tech at Comox at the time," says Arnie Macauley. "We got word from RCC that there was an aircraft down and that they had picked up an ELT hit. Later, one of our Auroras pinpointed the exact position of the crash, on the east side of a mountain, sixty miles or so from Vancouver. We learned later that the pilot had lost his engine in cloud because of carb ice and didn't make it through the mountains. He was on IFR at the time.

"The crash occurred late in the afternoon so there was no time to get in to the site before dark. We launched in a Lab at first light the next morning.

"I remember the pilot that day was Major Reg Lanthier. The other SAR Tech with me was George Makowski. We flew over to Vancouver and then up the Fraser Valley towards Harrison Hot

Springs. The weather was no hell anywhere, but the farther we went, the worse it got. Because the guys in the Aurora had located the crash, we knew exactly where we were going, but we just couldn't get there. The weather got worse and worse, and we'd try one valley, then another, but nothing worked. We actually spent a good part of the day doing this. Sometimes we would put down at logging camps and just wait for any clearing at all.

"Finally, fairly late in the afternoon we worked our way up to the base of the valley that they were in. A couple of media helicopters came in with us. However, it was still a while before we got a small break in the clouds. As soon as it came, we fired up right away."

Lanthier lifted the big Lab into the sky, and ever so slowly gained altitude. All the while, the ping of the ELT grew louder. Inside the rescue chopper, the men were really looking for wreckage now, because no one held out much hope of finding survivors. After all, it was twenty-four hours since the plane went down. Even if someone lived through the crash they would probably have perished from exposure after an entire night and a day on the mountain.

"We were still climbing," continues Macauley, "when we flew by something that stood out. I remember the flight engineer spotting the wreckage and saying 'Got 'em.' Then George, who was sitting at the right window, yelled, 'I see three survivors!' We told him he was crazy, but he said, 'No. There are three people down there waving out of a snow cave!' We could hardly believe it. They were on a sixty-degree snow slope, and it looked as if the airplane had crashed right into it. Then it had flipped upside down. It was obvious that there had been snow overnight and it looked as if there could be an avalanche at any minute. George and I wondered how in hell we were ever going to get them out of there."

Everyone on board the helicopter that day knew that if the people on the mountain were not removed right away, they would be dead in the morning. The very fact that they had survived to this point was, in itself, incredible. They had endured the crash, a major snowfall, subzero temperatures at the altitude where they were, and the imminent risk of avalanche. Another night would be unthinkable. In the meantime, the weather was closing in again.

"We first decided we'd get in as close as we could to the snow slope and hoist from there," explains Macauley. "So we pulled in to about a hundred yards from the mountain, but just got blasted out of there by downdraft. We peeled off and changed our plan. This time we decided to put on our mountain gear and have the helicopter put us down on the top of the mountain, and we would climb down to the crash from there. But the aircraft was right at its limit and there was so much turbulence up there it was hopeless. We had to pull out. Then we wondered about going down to the valley, dumping all of our extra equipment and trying with a lighter load. But then we realized with the size of the Lab there would be so much vibration and prop wash we could blow them right off the mountain and start an avalanche as well.

"Finally, we figured that if we had a helicopter that could hover at the altitude of the crash and create less turbulence, we might be able to get the people. So we called RCC and told them to find another helicopter right away. While they were doing that, we went back down to the valley.

"The CBC camera crew had their helicopter sitting there when we landed. One guy came over and asked if they could be of any help. We knew their aircraft was not big enough for what we needed, but I figured I could use it to have a better look at the crash site, to try to work out our next move. So the pilot kicked the cameraman out, and I hopped in. We hovered about a hundred feet in front of the crash, and I got a better look at it. I was also able to identify some features on the mountainside. As it turned out, we were damned lucky to get this second look because the weather was coming down and clouds were already back over the site."

Macauley and the pilot of the media helicopter then returned to what was becoming an impromptu base camp in the valley. They were barely there when another chopper came into view. This was the replacement aircraft which the RCC in Victoria had found on such short notice. The machine was owned by a B.C. company, Okanagan Helicopters, and was being flown by their chief test pilot, Terry Dixon. The plane itself was a Long Ranger, a more powerful version of the better known Jet Ranger. Fortuitously, the man flying it was said by some to be one of the best pilots they had ever seen. On this day, he would not only prove them right, he would demonstrate magnificent and cool-headed flying in a desperate situation.

"Terry shows up with the Long Ranger and a couple of slinging cables," Macauley goes on. "Fortunately, he had stopped in Abbotsford and picked up Craig Seager, another of our SAR Techs. We sure needed Craig, as it turned out. Anyway, we jury-rigged a Billy Pugh net [a large mesh scoop/cage rescue device] on a cable underneath the helicopter, and Craig Seager and George Makowski got in it. I rode in the cockpit to direct Terry.

"We took off, with the Billy Pugh hanging below us, and Craig and George swung out, three thousand feet or so over the valley. By this time the mountain was covered in cloud, there were ice crystals blowing around, and we could hardly see a damned thing. But we had all the luck in the world. I found this ridge of rock that I knew led up to where the people were, so we followed it and found them."

At the time Macauley located the ridge, the helicopter was slightly less than three hundred feet below the crash. In order to keep the cliff face in sight however, Dixon had to manoeuvre extremely close to it. This meant a slow, climbing hover with the tips of the whirling rotor blades sometimes only a foot from the mountainside. Had the machine accidentally drifted close enough for a blade to touch, the helicopter would have exploded in a fireball, the four would-be rescuers would have died in an instant, and the Ruwald party would have been still on the mountain. That afternoon Terry Dixon earned his pay.

Once during the slow nail-biting climb, the pilot turned to Macauley and said, "I'm getting nervous. Did you feel that?"

"Feel what?" the SAR Tech asked.

"My heart. When I'm nervous I can hear my heart pounding."

But Macauley later told the author that the chopper was steady as a rock; Dixon never for an instant lost his focus. He flew the plane, kept an eye on the rotors, and slowly climbed the cliff face immediately in front. Macauley did his best to look out for Seager and Makowski while watching the tail rotor so he could direct the pilot out if he lost reference. There was another ridge below and behind them and no-one wanted to hit it if they had to back off suddenly.

"Then Terry called, 'I've got it. I've got the crash site,'" Arnie Macauley remembers. "He tucked the plane in even closer it seemed and Craig and George were able to swing the net back and forth and jump onto the snow. They had their ice axes with them so they got a good grip. If they hadn't, they would have fallen all the way to the valley floor."

When Seager and Makowski reached the wreckage of the little Comanche, they found Bonnie Boucher and the Reiches alive, and considering their harrowing ordeal, in relatively good condition. All were lucid, even though Luke Reiche had suffered a broken arm when the plane hit the mountain. Sadly, pilot Mike Ruwald was dead.

As quickly as safety permitted, the SAR Techs on the snow strapped the two women into the rescue cage, Makowski held onto the side of it, and Dixon prepared to take the first load down. Seager remained at the crash site with Luke Reiche.

"Just getting out of there was dicey," Arnie Macauley recalls. "The cloud was like soup and we could hardly see a thing. Terry felt he couldn't just back down the mountain, but we had to back away from it. Then he did a pedal turn to his left while I tried to watch the ridge on our right. Finally we get out of there, popped through the cloud into clear air and whisked right down to the valley."

Once there, Makowski and Macauley put the two women into electric blankets in the waiting Labrador, and then returned for Reiche and Seager. Fortunately, the clouds had cleared.

Because the priority in Search and Rescue is to assist the living, the body of Mike Ruwald had to be left on the mountain while his friend, the injured Luke Reiche, was removed from it. By the time the Long Ranger was up to the crash site, Seager had put a splint on Reiche's arm, and he and Seager came down in the Bully Pugh. Then the three crash survivors were immediately taken in the Lab to a hospital in Abbotsford.

"We really admired those folks," Macauley told me. "They had some cuts and scrapes, and the broken arm, but after what they had been through, they were in pretty good shape. And they had done everything right. After the crash, they dug themselves the snow cave, then hauled seat cushions out of the airplane. They poured some oil over the cushions and kept a fire going for warmth. By doing all this, they had saved their own lives. But they were about at their wit's end when we got there. I'm sure they wouldn't have made it through another night. The oil was gone and they were already getting hypothermia and were starting to lose it."

The crash survivors were all treated at an Abbotsford hospital and then released. By chance, they ended up staying in the same hotel where the SAR Techs had rooms. In a way, this was fortuitous.

"Later that evening, I heard a tap on my door and when I opened it Bonnie Boucher was standing there," explains Macauley. "She told me the RCMP did not have the equipment to get her husband's body off the mountain until the weather was better, and she asked if we would bring him down for her. So George and I volunteered.

"The weather was good the next day, and this time Terry brought another pilot with him. George and I took some rescue tools and crash axes with us, and even then, it took us over an hour to get the body out. Because the plane had flipped when it crashed, it came down on Mr. Ruwald and had broken his neck. We actually had to cut through the floor to get to him. When we had the body ready to go, we collected it, the log books, the luggage and anything else of value and put everything into a big cargo net. Terry took this down first. Then he came back up with the Billy Pugh and George and I had a nice ride down."

The SAR Techs who received the Medal of Bravery for their role in rescuing survivors of a British Columbia mountain-top plane crash pose for a picture at Government House in Ottawa. They are (L to R): Arnie Macauley, George Makowski, and Craig Seager. (Canadian Forces photo)

*   *   *   *   *

Much later, on Friday, November 9, 1984, Arnie Macauley, George Makowski and Craig Seager stood in the palatial gold-and-cream ballroom at Rideau Hall in Ottawa and watched as Governor General Jeanne Sauve presented Terry Dixon with the Star of Courage for an act of "conspicuous courage in circumstances of great peril." The three admired what Dixon had done, and congratulated him for being a truly fine pilot. Then, a few minutes later, the Governor General bestowed the Medal of Bravery on the SAR Techs who had saved those three lives almost two years before.

11

Rescuing the Rescuer

Much of the land northwest of Thunder Bay, Ontario is wild, rugged, starkly beautiful, and to the outsider, incredibly lonely. It is a place of pine, rock, deer and deadwood. It is a land of lakes, lichen, forests and fish. It is home to the blackfly, the bear, the mosquito and the moose. And where human beings have gone, it is the place of the plane — on wheels, floats and skis. Indeed, without the plane, this near north would be deprived of its most vital, and in some cases only, link to the world away.

In summer and winter, bush planes crisscross the mind-numbing distances between towns so tiny they make Dryden and Kenora seem big. They carry people, freight, sometimes livestock, and food. And just as important, they bring those from elsewhere who fish and hunt and pay for their pleasures with money that reads "In God We Trust."

But while almost all flights are successful and routine, they sometimes end prematurely. Pilots have come down because of a host of factors: weather, lack of fuel, engine failure, disorientation, even their own stupidity.

On January 27, 1984, a man named John Zygmunt landed, not because he wanted to, but because the gasoline in his little Cessna 180 had been contaminated with water. As the motor sputtered alarmingly, and threatened to quit at any minute, the 24-year-old pilot set his machine down on the ice- and snow-covered surface of a lake without a name, far short of where he had planned on going.

Zygmunt was alone, roughly halfway between his departure point, Muskrat Dam, and his destination Stewart Lake, 250 miles or so south. He knew the country and because he did, a forced landing was not unduly alarming. He expected to be held up for a day or so, but knew he would be located sooner or later and clean fuel could be flown in. His landing was uneventful and his plane undamaged. In order to set the wheels in motion for his recovery, Zygmunt switched on the aircraft's ELT. Then he prepared for a night in the bush by building a fire and making himself as comfortable as he could. At no time did he panic.

Because Zygmunt had filed a flight plan, he was expected at Stewart Lake about mid-afternoon that Friday. When he was still not there at 7:30 P.M., the Ontario Provincial Police were informed. Sometime earlier however, a signal from his ELT was detected by a high flyer, a commercial aircraft that happened to be passing over that part of the province. The signal was reported to the Rescue Co-Ordination Centre in Edmonton, and in due course, a search was launched for the downed plane. Larry Scott and Bill Barber were the two SAR Techs on it. Scott was a SAR veteran, Barber a newcomer to the trade. They were from widely different backgrounds.

Calgary-born, and a former navy man, Scott was ten years older than Barber. His father, who had owned a construction company, was killed in a car accident when Larry was 7, and the son went away to sea because he could not get along with the man who would later become his stepfather. (Today, they are close.) Scott joined the navy because his father had once sailed.

Bill Barber was raised in Orangeville, Ontario, the second

oldest of six. His father was a firefighter. As a youngster, Barber played hockey, and was also goaltender on provincial championship lacrosse teams. After high school, he attended Ryerson in Toronto, where he majored in urban planning — not, he says today, something he uses very often as a SAR Tech.

"We took off about six o'clock, as I recall," Barber says of the Zygmunt search, "and it took us a while to get on scene. Once we were there though, we had no trouble finding the plane on the ground. As well as the ELT, the pilot had lit three fires out on the lake where he was. They were in the form of a triangle, the international distress signal. By this time, it was a little after midnight."

"The weather wasn't too bad," says Larry Scott. "There was a fairly stiff breeze though, and we knew there would be heavy snow on the ground. As it turned out, we were sure right about this. On the way from Edmonton, we got our gear ready in case we had to jump. At that time, we had no idea whether whomever was in the plane was alive or not.

"When we saw the three fires, we did a couple passes over the lake, but there was no sign of anybody around," Scott continues. "We didn't know if the guy was still in the plane, or where he was. Obviously somebody had been well enough to set out the fires though.

"But when we tried to raise him on the radio, there was no response. Then we came over again and dropped a small radio on a parachute. Again nothing."

"By now, we were starting to think maybe the person down there had been hurt, or was sick or something," Bill Barber adds. "That's when we made the decision to parachute down and check things out. Because of the kind of night it was, we decided not to use flares; instead we would jump to the fires. We dropped a rescue toboggan and went out after it. I was carrying our medical kit."

The SAR Techs jumped from eight hundred feet, off the ramp at the back of the Herc. Then the wind caught them and they drifted apart, out over the lake below. Both men estimate

Bill Barber jumps from the ramp of a Hercules. His jump from a similar aircraft to the frozen surface of a northern Ontario lake resulted in serious injuries to himself. The man he was going to help had sent out distress signals after his plane came down.

that they hit the ice at about thirty miles per hour. Larry Scott's landing was a good one.

"For a while I didn't know where Bill was," Scott says today. "I was first off the ramp and he was a little above me on the way down. When I landed, I was busy collapsing my chute and getting myself orientated, so I never saw him land. I just remember thinking how deep the damned snow was. But the next thing I knew, I heard Bill yelling somewhere in the darkness off to my left."

And Barber was yelling for good reason.

His descent from the plane had been fairly routine, but the heavy snow below him was a problem. Because he carried one hundred pounds or so of gear, including the medical kit on his back, Barber's feet and legs sank deep into a drift as soon as he touched. Unfortunately, at that precise moment, a strong gust of wind filled his parachute, and knocked him backwards, over the medical gear and into the snow. That single motion, which he says he will never forget, snapped his right thigh bone in seven places. Then the wind-filled parachute began dragging him through the snow.

"I had difficulty just holding on," he says, "but I was finally able to cut the canopy away and the dragging stopped. I knew I was still in big trouble though, because my right leg was draped back over my shoulder. I knew I couldn't just leave it there because I was afraid of femoral bleeding."

With a presence of mind and a display of raw courage truly unfathomable, Barber reached back over his shoulder, grabbed the cuff of his winter flight pants, and pulled. His grotesquely distorted right leg came down past his face, the grinding ends of the shattered bone audible in his ear. There was a moment of white-hot blinding pain that brought tears to his eyes, took his breath away, and left him fighting to remain conscious, staring at the stars. Then he leaned forward, twisted his leg into what looked like its proper alignment, and stretched it in front of him. He then took some of his parachute lines, wrapped them around his upper thigh and tightened them as much as he could bear, willing the makeshift tourniquet to work. Finally, exhausted, frightened and terribly alone, he lay back in the snow and called Larry Scott. Bill Barber's mission of mercy was truly over.

"It took me almost twenty minutes before I found Bill," Scott explains. "I got to Mr. Zygmunt afterwards, but as it turned out, he was not injured at all. He had heard our plane, but not the radio, and he didn't notice the one we dropped. Luckily, he was actually able to help me with Bill."

By this time it was about 1:30 A.M.

"As I was lying there in the snow, John Zygmunt came over to me and asked, 'Are you okay?'" laughs Bill Barber today. "I told him I was the one who was supposed to be asking that question.

"Anyway, Larry was excellent. He gave me a shot of morphine right away, then got the tent set up and me into it. He splinted my leg as best he could and put a pair of mast trousers on me. He heated water, started an IV in my arm to get some fluids into me, and remained there beside me all night. I know for certain that he saved my life, and I'll never forget him for doing so. He was always cheerful, helpful, and considerate. The guy is a real professional and a very fine human being. I know there is and always will be a bond between us."

The next day, Al McNeil of Sabourin Lake Airways out of

Cochenour, Ontario, was asked by the RCC to fly to the trio on
the ice and bring them out. He did so, on a ski-equipped, ten-
passenger Otter aircraft. By this time, Scott was out of morphine
for Barber, so the Otter went to a nursing station at Pickle Lake
for more. Zygmunt said his goodbyes there, and the two SAR
Techs were flown to Winnipeg where Barber was admitted to
hospital at the Health Sciences Centre. Finally, after extensive
reconstructive surgery, and several weeks recuperating in
Winnipeg, he was flown back to Edmonton.

"I'll never forget landing there," he explains. "The whole
section was out to meet me. That was a wonderful feeling,
because at the time of the accident I felt really bad, thinking I
had let all the guys down. I was new on the job then, and I
wanted to do it right and I'd screwed up. So it was great to see
everyone and have them let me know I was absolved, vindicated.
I was still a member of the SAR Tech family."

And there was another family glad to have Barber back. Bill
and his wife Lorrie had become the parents of twin boys not
long before the accident. (They already had a 3-year-old boy.)
With Bill in the hospital in Winnipeg and Lorrie at home with
three little people in Edmonton, her life was surely harried. Now
she looks back on that time as a bad dream.

A steel rod was inserted into Bill Barber's leg and wired into
place. Unfortunately, the rod has now come apart some three
inches from one end. Orthopaedic surgeons feel it should not be
worked on just now, but undoubtedly will have to be in the
future. In the meantime, Bill Barber still jumps from planes.

And all SAR Techs wear their medical kits out front.

12

Rooftop Rescue

It is closed now, but for almost five decades, there was an Air Force Base at Chatham, New Brunswick. It was located just outside of town, on Highway 11, so in all its years of operation people travelling down to Moncton, or on to Prince Edward Island, passed its gates. In times of crisis, the place was busy; there were military vehicles on the nearby roads, men and women in uniform everywhere, and aircraft of various types in the skies overhead. Then later, when the nation eased into more peaceful times, activity at Canadian Forces Base Chatham reflected the trend. A few planes still landed and left, but most of the time the place was quiet, as if poised to slip into the retirement that ultimately came.

But it was still operating on May 21, 1986, when a Search and Rescue Buffalo aircraft from 413 Squadron in Summerside, Prince Edward Island landed. The plane, flown by Major Gary Naylor, was on a training flight and had stopped at Chatham to pick up display materials for an upcoming air show. Among the crew members that day were two Search and Rescue

Technicians, Tom Elliott and Andy Morris. The two not only worked together, they had become friends as well, in part because they had arrived at Summerside at about the same time. Elliott's previous posting was at Comox, B.C., while Morris had been a SAR Tech in Edmonton. Both held the rank of corporal.

As the Buffalo landed at the base, a construction crew was busy building a new thermal power demonstration station in downtown Chatham, on the south bank of the Miramichi River. The thirty-three-million-dollar endeavour was an attempt to see if a combination of high-sulphur coal and oil shale could be burned to produce electricity, while still remaining within strict environmental guidelines. The plant itself would be owned by the New Brunswick Electric Power Commission, but financing was supplied in large part by the federal government. Construction had been underway for almost two years, and the plant was just short of its scheduled completion date. If the technology used in the demonstration plant worked, then New Brunswick Power was expected to consider building a large commercial-scale operation. In the meantime, work on the prototype continued.

On that May morning, several workers were in and near the motor control centre of the project when, without warning, an electrical arc caused a sudden explosion and flash fire. Almost instantly, searing flames engulfed the construction electrician who was closest to a panel where the trouble began. Although severely burned about the face and upper body, the man managed to tumble to safety, but the conflagration had already spread to insulating materials that lay nearby. In no time, it seemed, there was fire everywhere.

As soon as they realized what was happening, workers nearest the doors dashed outside. They brought the man who had been burned with them, and within minutes he was in an ambulance speeding to Hotel Dieu Hospital in town.

The Chatham Fire Department responded in force. A rescue vehicle and three pumpers were sent to the scene, and once there, firefighters donned air packs and dashed into the plant. At the time, an unknown number of men were trapped inside. No-one knew whether they were alive or dead.

Fortunately, the men were alive, but they were starting to wonder how long their luck would hold. They had escaped the fire, but then billows of acrid grey-white smoke spreading through the plant drove them away from the doors. In desperation, half-blinded, coughing, and holding handkerchiefs over their faces, the men retreated to a stairwell and struggled upwards until finally they spilled out onto the roof, more than three hundred feet above the ground. Even if no aerial ladder could reach this far, they could at least breathe the clear air. A light wind blew the smoke away from the roof.

Meanwhile, out at C.F.B. Chatham, the crew from Greenwood had finished loading the items they came for, and had stopped into a hangar snack bar for lunch. They were there when they heard about the fire.

"A flight engineer from the base noticed our Buffalo on the ramp and had gone to ask Major Naylor if there were SAR Techs on board," recalled Andy Morris. "The guy was directed to us. He told us there was a fire at a generating station downtown, and that there were people trapped on the roof. He wondered if we could help get them off. He said they had a Huey [helicopter] there that we could use, but no SAR Techs.

"We asked if the helicopter had a rescue hoist. When they said it did, Tom and I ran out to our own plane, grabbed a couple harnesses and some medical equipment and then went to the Huey. We were in the air in no time. I remember the pilot's name was Captain McLaughlin, a really relaxed guy."

The helicopter was scarcely airborne when the crew saw the smoke downtown. They flew directly towards it, and once there, did a quick orbit around the burning power plant.

"All we could see was this billowing smoke," said Morris. "It was pouring out of the building at the ground level, and also through the open door that came out onto the roof. At no time did we see any flames. Then as soon as we saw where the men were, we told the pilot what we wanted to do. The guy was great. He did everything we asked."

Far below, on the ground, the firefighters were picking their way through the area where the fire started, doing their best to contain it, hosing it down as they went. Because so many of the burning materials were chemicals — painted steel, insulated cables and the like — the smoke was extremely dense. Later on, Chatham Fire Chief James Currie reported that seven of his men had to be sent to Hotel Dieu for smoke inhalation. Fortunately, all were treated and released. Half a dozen construction workers also ended up at the same hospital, but apart from the man who was burned at the outset, injuries were non-life-threatening. (At the request of his family, the seriously burned gentleman's name was not made public.)

On the streets near the power plant, police kept the ever-increasing crowds back out of danger. Through traffic in the immediate area was curtailed, and a grassy area adjacent to a parking lot was cleared for use by the helicopter. As soon as word got around that men would be airlifted from the roof, concerned family members converged on the temporary helipad. There were many tearful reunions there once the rescue operation got underway.

SAR Tech Andy Morris helped in the helicopter rescue of fourteen men trapped on the roof of a burning power plant in Chatham, New Brunswick.

"There was quite a crowd watching the whole thing," Andy Morris remembers. "Of course, a fire is a big draw anyway, but when you have a large building, lots of smoke, police and several fire trucks, people tend to gather. I guess our helicopter added to the show.

"The power plant was a big concrete building with few windows, and the roof was flat, with a gravel top, and a railing around the outside. The men on the roof were at one end, away from the smoke. They were really orderly, although it was obvious they were pretty tense.

"We wanted to get one SAR Tech on the roof as soon as we could, to do a quick triage [system of priorities] if anyone was injured and to do some kind of prioritization as to who would go off the roof first. The helicopter hovered over the roof, and I went down first," Morris continues.

"I introduced myself to the guys, and then told them what we intended to do, and how it would be done. Tom came down with the horsecollar.

"There were no injuries, but a couple of fellows had been exposed to a lot of smoke. Tom took them up the hoist first because we were worried about them. The flight engineer helped them into the helicopter. I remained on the roof.

"In cases like this, we generally feel it is important for our SAR Techs to stay with whomever we are trying to rescue. They see right away that you are in the same situation as they are, and it has a calming effect. We also like to get people involved in their own rescue. In any group, there is generally somebody who takes charge: a boss, a foreman, the oldest there, and so on. If they are organizing themselves, it keeps them busy, and they don't tend to just wait and worry.

"It is also better to have the helicopter hover, preferably with the people being hoisted directly underneath. In cases like that they're not exposed to prop wash in the same way as they would be if the chopper was off to one side. The area directly underneath is calm, like the eye of a hurricane.

"It is also better to hover over a roof, and hoist from there.

Then the person being taken up is not as nervous because the roof is right underneath. If we'd done the hoisting off to one side, the person in the collar would get lifted off the roof, and then suddenly he would be three hundred feet in the air. That's a bit scary for some people."

The Huey remained about twenty-five feet from the rooftop during the evacuation. In all, fourteen men were rescued, in three flights, because the helicopter was not large enough to bring everyone down at once. For each flight, the men were hoisted on board, the door was closed and the aircraft dropped to the lawn below. Then the process was repeated. When the last of the stranded hydro workers were safely on board, the SAR Techs left as well. Tom Elliott came last.

"The entire rescue took only about ten minutes," Andy Morris explained. "Then we flew back to the base, got cleaned up a bit and finished our lunch. We were about to leave for home when another call came in. Would we do a medivac right away?"

This time, the call involved the man who had been burned so severely in the plant fire.

"We set up our IVs on the Buffalo," Morris says. "The oxygen system was ready to go as well, when an ambulance arrived from a local hospital. The poor guy was taken on board, and a doctor and nurse came along. We flew them down to Fredericton."

The burn victim was rushed to the Everett Chalmers Hospital in the provincial capital, the doctor and nurse from Chatham were flown back, and the Buffalo from Summerside headed home.

Lunch was over.

13

Diver Down

Steve Sykes had done this job before. It meant that early in the morning, he and two men he knew and trusted would climb into a truck in Hamilton. Then they would drive north for a couple of hours to the Muskoka Lakes district of Ontario, to a power plant and dam on the beautiful Severn River, fifteen miles northwest of Orillia. There, Sykes would put on a diving suit and enter a water-filled chamber inside the dam, do some repairs, and climb back out. Then he would take off his diving gear, load it up, and the trio would depart. The job might take half a day at most, and although it involved an element of danger, it was generally fairly routine.

But not always.

In fact, on the July 16, 1991, Steve Sykes almost died at the dam.

The 31-year-old was from Toronto, where he had been raised by his mother following the death of his father some time earlier. He was a professional diver, and a graduate of the Seneca College dive program. Now however, his water work was done

Will Bruce, left, and Mike Simpson used all their diving skills to rescue Steve Sykes, below, from certain death at the bottom of a power dam near Orillia, Ontario.

when he had a day or two off from his regular job as a city firefighter.

"When you work for a fire department, you have rather strange hours," he says, "so every time I had the chance I would do some diving for a company in Hamilton, Soderholm Marine Services. I had done a lot of stuff for them in the past, and I enjoyed it. The boss there, Leif Soderholm, asked me if I would go up to Muskoka and do some work on a dam for the Orillia Water, Light and Power Commission. I said, 'Sure.'"

So it was that shortly after 9:00 A.M. on that warm, sunny Tuesday, Sykes and the two men with him, Dave Babcock and Dave Devalk, pulled their van up beside the Swift Rapids Generating Station, one of three such operations belonging to Orillia Power. On the way from Hamilton, the dive crew had discussed what they would be doing; and once on site, they were given final information for the task.

"The people there told us they were losing hydraulic fluid in one of the lines going to a dam gate," Sykes recalls. "They wanted us to go down and try to find the leak and repair it. The job seemed fairly straightforward at the time.

"The idea was that I would dive into the chamber behind the gate, and then air would be pumped down the hydraulic line. The air would escape wherever the break in the line was, and I would essentially follow the bubbles to see where repairs had to be made."

The place where Sykes would work was only a part of a much larger complex. In addition to the dam and power plant, Swift Rapids included a canal lock, a huge, reinforced concrete structure familiar to boaters using the Trent-Severn waterway system.

The particular dam chamber Sykes would enter was in essence a large water-filled concrete vault, about fifty feet deep. On the downriver wall of the vault, near the bottom, was a ten ton steel door called a headgate, which could be raised and lowered to either stop the water or let it flow through the dam, into the power-generating turbines immediately adjacent. Because of the break in the hydraulic line (which was essential to its operation), the headgate could not be moved; it was stuck in the "down" position.

Before going into the water, Sykes went over the procedure with his crew. His backup that day was Dave Babcock, also a diver, and now fully suited and ready to enter the vault should Sykes run into trouble. Dave Devalk, the third team member, was called the tender. He looked after the umbilical, or lifeline that linked Sykes to the surface. It was a combination of safety rope, air line, and communications wire. The three were taped together, and payed out to Sykes as he descended. Tender and diver were in radio contact at all times.

"It was almost mid-morning by the time I was ready to go into the water," Sykes recalls. "That's when the dam operators assured me the gate was closed and everything was in place. As soon as they had air flowing through the line, I went into the chamber. I could see the bubbles and I began to follow the hydraulic line down to check where they were coming from. There was also some oil in the water.

"There was a bit of light near the surface, coming from the opening at the top of the chamber. However, as I went down, the light got dimmer and dimmer, until everything was black. I had a light on my helmet, a very bright sabre light, but that was it."

On the downriver side of the vault, just above the headgate, was a large, curved concrete abutment. It facilitated the downward flow of water, and encased the headgate when the barrier was raised. Sykes swam down to the abutment, and then, realizing that the bubbles were coming from below it, made his way lower.

"At this point, I couldn't detect any change in pressure," he recalls. "Nor did there seem to be any water flow at all."

Then he went deeper, by this time close to forty feet under water. As he did so, he kept his eye on the bubbles, all the while feeling the wall of the abutment as he descended. When he reached the bottom of it, he moved in for a closer look; his light swept along the floor of the chamber, and then to the great metal bulk of the headgate. His umbilical snaked below him.

An aerial view of the Swift Rapids generating station in winter. It was deep inside a chamber here where diver Steve Sykes was trapped. (Photo courtesy Brian Burnie and Orillia Water, Light & Power Commission)

The Swift Rapids generating station from below the dam. Deep under water in a chamber here was where diver Steve Sykes was trapped. (Photo courtesy of Brian Burnie and Orillia Water, Light & Power Commission)

"Ordinarily, the umbilical is almost neutral in buoyancy," Sykes explains. "It kind of floats along with you as you descend, and the tender feeds you line as you need it. You don't want the line too slack, but neither do you want it too tight. You don't want to keep saying, 'Give me slack, give me slack,' all the time. For the tender, it's a bit like lowering a rock on a rope. He can feel the tension, and goes with it. Then when the diver gets to wherever he's going to work, the tender allows a bit extra so the person in the water is not hampered in whatever he's doing."

Up on top of the dam, tender Devalk could feel the tension on the line, and allowed more and more of it into the chamber. Soon he knew Sykes had to be down about as far as he would be going.

Yet the line was still taut.

"At about that point, I was right at the bottom," Sykes continues, "and I turned to check my umbilical."

The diver will never forget what he saw.

The line leading away from him was tight, and instead of drifting or even floating upwards, was being pulled down. When he went to see why, he realized, to his horror, that the umbilical was being drawn towards the bottom because the headgate was not completely closed. To make matters worse, the umbilical was being sucked underneath!

"I yelled at Dave, 'Pull up! Pull up!'" said Sykes. "I told him what had happened, but he couldn't pull up. The water pressure right at the bottom was unbelievable. The gate was open about three to five inches or so because — as we learned later — some rocks had become wedged under it."

While Devalk, and then Devalk and Babcock together, struggled with the line, desperately trying to raise it, Sykes attempted to help himself. He inched closer to the gate, braced himself against it, and reached to pull his umbilical free.

Doing so almost killed him.

The tremendous and deadly pressure of water being forced through the tiny opening hit Sykes from behind and slammed him hard against the steel door in front of his face. His hands, both on the umbilical, were yanked forward and drawn into the outflow, momentarily trapping him. He tried to pull back, but it was only after the water had ripped off both his gloves that he succeeded. However, the motion caused his right knee, and then his outstretched left leg, to become wedged in the space below the headgate. Fortunately, neither went right under it.

"I realized right then that I was trapped," says Sykes, as the memory flashes across his face. "I knew it was about fifty feet up to the hatch opening, and that I was under about forty-five feet of water. I figured getting out of here would likely be chancey, but I still wasn't about to give up.

"After I collected my thoughts, I told the surface to send me down another line so I could attach it to one of the D-rings on my harness and maybe they could pull me up. When it came down, I hooked it on and then they tried — a couple of times. But it didn't work. Even with my harness on, the top of my body was being pulled, but my legs were not moving. I had a lot of pain from that, and I knew if they continued, they would have killed me. They would have pulled my body apart. I told them to tie the line tight, though, because it held me up.

"The best way to describe my position is that I was kneeling, facing right up against the gate, my right knee trapped by the pressure, and my left leg more or less stretched out, wedged into the space below the gate. The force of the water made it impossible for me to move either of my legs — even a fraction of an inch. The line from the surface held me upright, so I was pretty much kneeling all the time I was in there."

Up on the surface, Babcock was about to go into the chamber to help his friend, but Sykes was firm in insisting that he not do so. One diver in trouble was enough, and in any event, Babcock would not be able to help if he did come down. In fact, there was a real danger that he too would be trapped in the same way. Reluctantly Babcock agreed, and from then on, he, Devalk and the Orillia Power employees present wracked their brains in a desperate attempt to come up with a way to free the diver. They refused to acknowledge the alternative....

In the meantime, Steve Sykes knelt against the steel door far below, in the oily blackness of what he was beginning to fear was his tomb. In order to save power, he turned off his dive light because even with it, little was visible. And perhaps not being able to see was better anyway.

"I really thought I was going to die there," he admits. "In fact, from the moment I was sucked in, I pretty well knew I was done. I decided that if this was my time, then it was; I had no regrets. I was content with the way I had lived my life, and I had pretty much done what I wanted. I'm not a religious person, so I didn't pray. Instead, I thought of my mother and my sister and my nephew and of the good relationship I'd had with all of them.

"I didn't have a watch on, so I had no idea of time. There was really no need to know because time was at a standstill for me anyway. I never knew how long I'd been there, but I remember the first while being the worst. I was in unbelievable pain, and the position I was in didn't help. But then, I started to lose all sensation in my legs, until eventually I could not feel anything from my waist down. About that time I realized that if I ever did get out, I would probably be paralyzed, so my life was going to be changed no matter what.

"One of the first rules of either commercial diving or scuba diving is to not panic if you get in trouble. That's easier said than done, but I forced myself to remain calm. Being able to talk to the surface helped. I knew they were doing everything they could for me."

And they were.

In short order, OPP officers were on the scene, as were firefighters, ambulance attendants, local emergency measures officials, and technical experts from the Orillia Water, Light and Power Commission. Among the latter were John Mattinson, an electrical engineer, and Brian Burnie, a designer draftsman. Their expertise and knowledge of the workings of the generating station proved invaluable. However, no-one had been able to come up with a way to free Steve Sykes.

Someone mentioned Search and Rescue.

"I certainly remember the call," says Lieutenant-Colonel Rick Hardy, who was at the Rescue Co-Ordination Centre in Trenton that day. "We spend most of our time jumping to plane crashes and hauling people off sinking ships and so on, and this thing was a bit different, but we responded as soon as we could. Luckily, we had a helicopter and some guys in wetsuits training in the Bay of Quinte at the time, so they were tasked to Muskoka immediately."

"There was a lot of confusion, and quite a crowd had gathered when we landed," SAR Tech leader Mike Simpson said. "I was on Rescue 308. Steve Ackland was the other SAR Tech with me, and we knew another Lab with three more of our guys was on the way. As it turned out, we needed everybody.

"I remember wondering what in hell we were in for," he continues. "Neither Steve nor I knew anything about this kind of thing, so we needed a crash course in how the dam worked. The technology was from 1915 or something. One of the engineers there told us the gauges they used showed that the gate was closed, but that debris was apparently under it. That's why the guy was trapped in the first place.

"Luckily for us — and for him — Mr. Sykes did not panic. He was terrific, and really helpful. I had an awful lot of admiration for him, because he was really brave. We were able to talk to him and monitor his condition, and what it was like down there. I'm sure he was aware of the stats for survival though. A bystander told us there had been several incidents like this in the previous five years, but in every case, the diver had died. That sure didn't raise our morale much.

"In the helicopter on the way to the site, I had been in radio contact with the DCIEM [Defence and Civil Institute of Environmental Medicine] in Toronto, and with Toronto General Hospital. The doctors had told us that even if we were able to get the victim free right away, he would have to remain at a depth of ten feet for thirty minutes in order to decompress. If not, he could die from the bends. That had to be kept in mind as we worked.

"I remember looking down through the opening in the top of the dam, and all I could see was black, oily water. I knew the people there were pretty frustrated and I asked what they had tried so far. As they told me, I thought each idea they'd come up with was good and I would have done the same things. Only none of them had worked. So, no matter what Mr. Sykes said, I knew we would have to go down inside. By this time, our second helicopter arrived on scene, and Marty Maloney, Will Bruce and Brian Weir were in it. I told them what we were up against."

From this time on, an increasingly important part of the underwater chamber would be what was called its stoplog wall. Located upriver, about thirty feet from the headgate side, and made of large, wooden beams placed on top of one another, the wall functioned as the initial control mechanism for the amount of water passing through the dam. In essence, the more logs in place, the less water moved through. Ordinarily, when the chamber where Steve Sykes was trapped was empty, the stoplogs held back virtually all the water coming down. On this day, however, because the chamber had been already full of water, beams placed in the stoplog wall would not seal themselves, so water gushed through between them. The gaps had to be closed somehow.

The idea of sealing the cracks between the logs had been considered almost from the beginning of the emergency, but no reliable way to do so had been found. But then, during a frenzied period of brainstorming, somebody wondered aloud about maybe some big tarps...

The question quickly became the answer.

The firefighters located two very large canvas tarps and lots of sandbags. In using both, the rescuers felt, there finally might just be a ray of hope.

"Steve Ackland and I got into the water above the stoplogs," Mike Simpson explains, "and the folks there hauled the tarps up onto the dam and then lowered them down to us. The three SAR Techs who had just arrived acted as tenders while we did the diving."

Ackland and Simpson draped the tarps, one after the other, down over the wooden wall. Then they heaped sand bags on the bottom fringes, ensuring that these would remain tight against the logs. The pressure of the river flow also helped to flatten the canvas in place. Additional sandbags on the dam kept the top edges of the tarps from being dragged down by the current. Finally, when they had done all they could in the water, the divers climbed out. The entire operation had taken about forty-five minutes.

Fortunately, it would prove successful. The water in the chamber began to drop.

"It wasn't very fast," says Mike Simpson, "but it was dropping maybe three inches a minute. The dam operators told us the chamber was narrower down farther, so we figured the drop would speed up eventually. In the meantime, we were concerned for Mr. Sykes."

"I knew when I began my dive that none of the logs had been in," Steve Sykes told the author, "but Dave Devalk said they were put in after I got trapped. Then when I heard they had some tarps holding the water back, I felt better. I knew that if this worked, then it would be just a waiting game for the water drop. I was glad the SAR Techs were there, and I was really impressed by everything they did that day."

"From time to time, Mr. Sykes reported feeling nauseous, and that was a constant worry," Mike Simpson continues. "We were afraid he might throw up, and that would have really complicated things. As it was, we were feeding him oxygen to reduce his chances of decompression sickness if he had to be removed quickly. At one stage, the doctors told us if we pulled him out too fast, we would need to re-submerge him upriver at a ten foot depth for forty-five minutes. However, that never happened. The water level went down slowly enough, and as it did DCIEM ran repeated dive profiles until they eventually determined decompression would no longer be required. Believe me, that was a relief.

"Despite the fact that Mr. Sykes warned us not to dive down

to him, we felt we had to in order to see what we faced. Marty Maloney and Will Bruce put on scuba gear and went into the vault. Steve Ackland and I stayed on top to co-ordinate things as best we could."

Situation reports covering these moments reveal that the rescue teams on the top of the dam were under the impression that Steve Sykes' feet had actually passed under the headgate. For this reason, they feared the gate could suddenly work itself loose and crash down, severing the diver's legs. Because of that possibility, every effort was made to secure the gate in its present position. That involved diving down inside the headgate abutment and attaching cables to metal rings found on the top corners of the gate itself. These dives, fraught with extreme danger, were made by Will Bruce, with Maloney acting as his safety man. Bruce went down alone, headfirst, in total darkness, into a space that was barely wider than his shoulders. Eventually though, the cables were connected to the rings, and then in turn hooked to a crane boom on the surface. The crane, however, could only lift about two and a half tons, and was far too small to hoist the ten-ton gate. For this reason, a complicated mechanical advantage rope and pulley system was put in position for added security in case the gate moved. All five SAR Techs were assisted in this installation by local firefighters.

And gradually, the water level in the chamber dropped — finally enough that it was felt to be safe for someone to check the trapped diver. Will Bruce did so, supported by Brian Weir. The latter also took a small hydraulic jack down with him. There was some hope that the device could be wedged under the headgate in order to raise it, but the jack was half an inch too high. Bruce did a blind physical examination of Steve Sykes but remained in the vault — at the water's surface.

"As the water level dropped, I started to feel a decrease in pressure," says Sykes. "I remember putting my hands down to try to free my legs, but not being able to do so. But a bit later, when I did the same thing with my hose, it came out a little. I pulled more of it back, and more came. Then I tried my legs again and they came. I was free!

"I backed away from the gate and told the surface I was out. Two seconds later, the SAR Techs grabbed me, but by then I don't think I was really with it. It had been a long time....

"I know they got me into a scoop stretcher which they had tied to the crane up top. Then one of them hooked himself to the stretcher and both of us were hoisted out.

"Then the pain hit me. I guess my circulation was coming back because I felt intense pain and a lot of nausea. I was given both morphine and gravol and then wheeled across the dam to an air ambulance. The next thing I knew, it was three days later and I was in Toronto, in a bed at Sunnybrook Hospital."

*   *   *   *   *

It was 4:46 P.M. when Steve Sykes was lifted from the dam chamber — more than six hours after he entered it. As a result of his near-death ordeal, his condition was still listed as serious following several days in the hospital. He had developed gas gangrene in his left leg, and the infection threatened to spread. It was only after Sykes was airlifted to Fillmore Hospital in Buffalo, New York and subjected to concentrated and invasive treatment there that the disease was contained and his condition improved. Then there were more operations, weeks of rehabilitation, and months away from work. Now however, Sykes has returned to the fire department, and has regained his exuberant cheerfulness and love of life. He is able to walk, run, and swim, and intends to dive again for sure — but perhaps not at the Swift Rapids dam.

SAR Techs are the most highly decorated group in the Canadian Armed Forces. This photo is of the men who won bravery awards following the disastrous Hercules crash at Alert in 1991. They are, left to right, back row: Derek Curtis, Rob Walker, Mark Lessard, Bruce Best, Jean Tremblay, Jim Brown, Al Houle, Bob Mondeville, Arnie Macauley, Fred Ritchie. Front row: Darby Darbyson, Ben House, Jean Roy, Ron O'Reilly, Gerry Dominie, Keith McKellar, Eric Larouche, Shawn MacDiarmid.

14

Crash at the Top of the World

On the last morning of July, 1950, a Royal Canadian Air Force Lancaster bomber prepared to drop supplies by parachute to the northernmost settlement on earth. The place was called Alert, a military listening post on Ellesmere Island, five hundred miles from the North Pole. The plane involved was from 405 Squadron in Greenwood, Nova Scotia, and was flown by D.T. French. Wing Commander French had eight officers and men with him.

The crew on the Lanc expected to be over the drop zone for only a few minutes before flying back to Thule, an American air base on the northwest coast of Greenland. Thule was used then, and still is, as the jumping-off point for the transport of supplies to the listening station. It was a larger and much less forbidding outpost than Alert itself. The men on the plane would be glad to get back there.

On the ground below the Lanc, the crew who would collect the delivery waited in anticipation, and watched as the four-engine aircraft approached. They saw the cargo doors part, some

151

thousand feet above them, then noticed a bundle come out. A parachute appeared.

Somehow, inexplicably, the chute failed to open.

As the horrified spectators looked on, it streamed back towards the rear of the plane, became entangled in the tail elevators, and remained caught there.

The effect on the bomber was immediate.

It lost altitude, veered out of control, and in a matter of seconds, plunged headlong onto the rock and permafrost below. All on board died instantly in the explosion and fire that followed.

One of those was a young flying officer named Everett McCutcheon of Cornwall, Ontario. He was stationed in Greenwood then, with his wife Joan, who was pregnant, and their little daughter, Gail. Gail now had one parent, Joan was a widow, and a second daughter Ann, born some months afterwards, would never see her father. Yet much later, both girls would see firsthand the place where this man that neither knew was killed.

Exactly thirty years from the date of the crash — on July 31,1980 — another aircraft flew over the northern outpost. This time, it was a Hercules from Ottawa, via Thule, carrying a handful of relatives of the men who had died so long before. Among the passengers were Gail and Ann McCutcheon, now married and accompanied by their husbands.

"The plane landed at Alert," says Carl Brand, who was married to Ann. "We were there for a memorial service for the deceased, so we were able to visit their graves and see the stone cairn which had been erected in their memory. It was very moving to honour the memories of those airmen who had sacrificed their lives at our northernmost frontier. The Hercules we went in on did a flypast, as an Air Force general said a few words. Then we were given a reception in the Officers' Mess and flew out."

But the legacy of Alert did not end with the crash of 1950, nor with its remembrance thirty years later. Unfortunately, this most desolate of locales was the scene of another tragedy, this time in 1991. In this catastrophe, five young people would die and several others would be scarred for life, but a third group would demonstrate that even in times of the most devastating heartbreak, genuine, unselfish heroism often comes to the fore. It certainly did in the twenty-four-hour darkness and bitter cold of the High Arctic on October 30, 1991, when a Hercules with eighteen people on board went down.

The plane was carrying a tank of diesel fuel to Alert, along with thirteen passengers, but unlike the situation in 1950, it would be landing at the northern base. There it would be unloaded, the passengers would climb out, and the aircraft would depart.

The supply-delivery procedure was quite different from that of earlier years. Now there were three planes ferrying material. All of it came from Thule, where it had been shipped by boat from southern Canada the previous summer. This Thule-Alert operation was a continuous one, yet always subject to interruption because of the changeable polar weather. In the best of all possible worlds, delivery took about ten days in total. "Boxtop" was the code name for these flights.

Shortly before 4:30 P.M. local time on October 30, Hercules 322, or Boxtop 22, was inbound from Thule. At the controls was 32-year-old John Couch, a Gulf War veteran and a seasoned Herc pilot. There were four crew members with him, along with the passengers. Aside from the personal belongings of the people on board, the load was fuel. It was carried in an internal tank in the cargo compartment of the plane. This "wet lift," as it was called, amounted to 3,300 Imperial gallons, weighing just over 28,000 pounds. In addition, there were about 24,000 pounds of aircraft fuel on board, and this, added to the wet lift, made the total weight of the plane almost 135,000 pounds.

The flight for the most part was routine. The weather was good, with visibility for as much as fifteen miles or more. There was no sun, of course, because at Alert there is total darkness from mid-October until March. On the ground, the temperature was twenty-two degrees Celsius below zero, with light winds.

As the Herc neared its destination, Couch talked to the control tower at Alert and assured himself that all was well for landing. He was given the temperature, the winds and their direction, and the visibility on the ground. And, because he could already see the runway lights in the distance, Couch opted for a visual approach.

This decision was unfortunate.

A dozen or so miles from touchdown, the crew apparently thought they were coming in above the frozen surface of the Lincoln Sea, immediately adjacent to the airstrip at Alert. Instead, they were over land that was dotted with hills. But by this time the plane was low — so low, in fact, that it hit one of the hills. The flight was over.

The port wing touched the ground first. This caused the plane to lurch to the left, break apart, and scatter itself in a crude semicircle across a shallow depression surrounded by outcrops of rock. The earsplitting screech of tearing metal cut the frozen silence, only to be followed by the explosion of aviation gasoline and the roar of a fire, fed by liquid oxygen that ignited in the cockpit. Already, all four of the plane's propellers had been ripped off, as the engines on which they had been mounted ground into the ice and stone.

The wings of the plane came to rest in one place, the tail in another, and the cockpit in a third. Human beings, living and dead, were tossed into the snow, then drenched in a massive gush of reeking diesel oil as the wet tank tore from its mounts and broke apart. Roaring flames lit the daytime darkness and billows of black smoke rose into the Arctic sky. Much of the plane was quickly reduced to charred rubber, melted metal and grotesque chunks of debris that defied description. Boxtop 22 was no more.

But here and there in this unspeakable hell were survivors, men and women who had trouble believing they were actually alive: a couple near the cockpit, others back of the wings, two in the oil- soaked snow some distance to one side. All were stunned at the suddenness of events, the chaos around them, and the terrible realization that the plane had just crashed.

Some got their bearings before others. Some were hurt more than others. Some could move and at least two could not — at least not on their own. Some would never move again.

The inside rear area of a Hercules aircraft. It was in a similar section of the downed plane where several survivors of the Alert crash were found.

News of the crash travelled fast. When Boxtop 22 did not touch down at Alert at 4:30 as expected, and could not be seen on approach, the radar operator attempted to locate it. The last contact had been a few miles out, but after that, there was nothing. Because Boxtop 21 was also en route to Alert, it was directed to the last known position of the missing plane.

At 4:50, the crew on the second Herc saw fires on the ground. Ten minutes later, Search and Rescue was notified.

*   *   *   *   *

Twenty-six hundred miles away, in Greenwood, Nova Scotia, Warrant Officer Arnie Macauley had just sat down to dinner. He was bone tired, and happy to be home after a long day. For more than seven hours he had been bouncing around in the back of a Hercules C-130, trying to keep an eye on a twenty-eight-man Japanese fishing vessel called the *Eishin Maru*. The ship was attempting to ride out a vicious Atlantic storm, ninety miles off Sable Island. In time, it did; the gale

These three men risked their lives by jumping into the teeth of a polar storm to save lives following the terrible crash of an aircraft in one of the most remote places on earth. They are (clockwise from top left): Arnie Macauley, Darby Darbyson, and Ron O'Reilly.

abated, and the trawler and its company moved on.

Twenty-nine-year-old Ron O'Reilly had been with Macauley. He too had been glad to wind down at the end of the day, playing with his daughter and admiring her Hallowe'en costume. He had just finished eating.

Both of these men were SAR Techs attached to 413 Squadron in Greenwood. Macauley, from Medicine Hat, was the team leader. O'Reilly, originally from North Vancouver, had come to Greenwood after the Canadian Forces Base at Summerside, P.E.I. had closed down.

The two men were personable, athletic, and veterans in their chosen profession. They loved being SAR Techs.

"I was still eating when my brother Marvin phoned," says Arnie Macauley today. "All he said was, 'There's a Herc down up in Alert. Get everybody in. It looks as if it's a MAJAID.'" Macauley's younger brother Marv was a Search and Rescue Hercules pilot at Greenwood; the "MAJAID" he referred to was a military code term for "Major Air Disaster," meaning the crash of an aircraft with more than ten people on board. Arnie kissed his wife Darlene and raced out the door.

"One of the guys at work called me," Ron O'Reilly remembers. "He said there was a Herc down up north and that they needed us all in. At first I thought he was pulling my leg, but he said, 'No, it's for real.' I got dressed and broke a land speed record getting in. I lived close to the base at the time."

While these two men in Nova Scotia were hearing the bad news from Alert, SAR Techs three time zones away were getting a similar message.

"It was just after 3:30 in Edmonton," says Darby Darbyson, who was at the Search and Rescue unit there. "Jim Brown and I were on standby duty on the Herc. We were in the SAR Tech room at the base and he said to me, 'Well, when are we going to get launched?' I knew he was just joking around, so I said, 'By four.' I had hardly said it when the buzzer went off. We jumped up and went right over to the Ops [Operations] Room in another hangar to find out what was going on. The guy I talked to said, 'Get on your plane right now. There's a Herc down at Alert.' I asked how many people were on board, because I knew there were often passengers going up there. He looked at me and then said, 'It doesn't matter. Just get on the aircraft!'

"I said, 'No, we've got to know. How many passengers are on board?' Finally the guy said, 'Wait here. I'll find out.' Then he came back and told me there were five aircrew and thirteen passengers. I was stunned ..."

In no time, every Search and Rescue squadron in Canada knew something was seriously wrong in the far north. The news that the plane had been overdue was one thing, but the alarming message that fires had been seen shocked everyone. Each person who heard the news understood, deep down, that a plane crash followed by a fire often, too often, meant no-one had survived.

And the arrival time for a rescue mission at Alert was anything but immediate. There were no helicopters there, and the place was far away from all the major SAR establishments in the south. Nevertheless, men and equipment were launched from Greenwood, Gander, Trenton and Edmonton, and later even Iceland and Alaska. The first to go were helicopters from Trenton and Gander respectively, but shortly afterwards, fully loaded Hercules rescue planes from Edmonton and Greenwood were in the air as well. The Edmonton contingent was about forty minutes ahead of Greenwood.

Every person flying to Alert that night knew the distances involved. The northern facility is about 2,500 miles from Moscow, for example, but close to 3,000 from Toronto. Just getting there by Herc would take a long time: roughly seven and a half hours from Greenwood, a little less from Edmonton. Once airborne, the rescuers would have plenty of time to contemplate what had to be done.

"I called Fred Ritchie, our team leader, at home," recalls Darby Darbyson, "and told him what we'd heard. He knew we were going to need a lot of people up there, so he put the MAJAID plan into effect. Then we called every SAR Tech we could find. In no time, the guys were streaming in, and the plane was loaded. Once everyone was accounted for, we left. There were twelve SAR Techs on board. Flying weather out of Edmonton was good; cool and clear."

The situation was much the same at Greenwood.

"As soon as I got to the base, I started opening up the shop and turning on the lights," said Ron O'Reilly. "As I went to get radios and stuff, it just seemed like a stream of orange [the colour of the SAR Tech uniform] coming in. It was amazing because it was rare for everyone in the Squadron to be around at the same time — there would be guys training somewhere else, and things, but when this call came in, just about everyone was there. We formed ourselves into a line, passing gear along and loading the Herc. At this point, we still did not have much information about the crash, so we were preparing for all possibilities. As we loaded what we thought we might need, the Techs on the floor were doing the fueling, and the pilots their flight planning.

"On the way north, we were still getting little bits of information, but not a lot. We learned that there was another Herc from Edmonton on the way, and we were calculating who would get there first. When we realized they would get there about an hour before us, we pretty much accepted that. Then later, when we heard that the weather was getting bad at Alert and that we likely would be part of the search, we started getting excited again. But we were really beginning to realize that this could be a long, hard job."

"The lack of information was a problem at first," explains Greenwood team leader Arnie Macauley. "For instance, we knew there'd been a crash, and that someone had seen flares near it, but at one point we were told that the plane might be down on the pack ice, and that there could be open water, so that meant we had to bring equipment for a water rescue, along with all the Arctic gear. We also loaded toboggans, water, personal survival kits, flares, drop lights, parachutes — everything we thought we might need.

"In all, we had fourteen SAR Techs on board when we left," Macauley continues. "I left four behind on standby.

"Because we knew the flight would be long, our first priority was to let everyone get some sleep, because most of us were dead tired when we started. And we knew, once we got there, we would be busy. The idea was to let everyone sleep as best they could until we were about three hours out, and then get them up and get our gear ready. We had to get the jump gear ready, the drop gear organized, and everyone had to be fed as well. We knew we were going to get up there in the middle of the night. The loadmaster started preparing meals when we were about three hours out. On the way up I stayed with my brother, who was flying the plane. There was a lot of radio communication back and forth and I wanted to monitor it so I could keep my guys informed as best I could.

"We knew as we went along that Edmonton was on the way as well, and that their ETA [Estimated Time of Arrival] would be an hour before us. We figured then that by the time we got there, Fred Ritchie would have a bunch of guys on the ground, so we began concentrating on camp gear and so on."

Meanwhile, on the Edmonton flight, things were progressing as well. Darby Darbyson takes up the story: "We spent quite a bit of time dividing up people and sorting equipment. There was the medical team, then the guys who would drop the equipment. After it was out, they would jump in as well.

"But about an hour out of Edmonton, we were told that a storm was approaching Alert. Then by the time we got there, the weather was really bad. It was storming, the clouds were low, and you couldn't see a thing. We flew over where we thought the crash was, several times, but nothing was visible on the ground. We threw out flares but they didn't help at all. They just reflected off the clouds. You'd throw a flare, turn away for a second, and when you looked back, you couldn't see the flare. It was very windy, snowing heavily, and when we had the ramp down at the back, really cold."

When all efforts in the air seemed futile, the plane landed at

Alert in order to either wait out the storm, or at least see if there might be a break in it. Then, once on the ground, Fred Ritchie decided to split his team. He and others would try to get to the downed plane by tracked vehicle. An earlier attempt to do this by base personnel had failed when they were stymied by a huge gorge bordering the Sheridan River, southeast of Alert and tantalizingly close to the crash site. Ritchie resolved to try another route, closer to the sea. The second half of his crew would go back out in the air if the weather improved.

While all this was happening, the plane from Greenwood neared its objective.

"When the time came, we woke the guys," said Arnie Macauley, "and when we were about an hour out of Alert, we heard what was going on there. We were expecting to hear notice of a crash location, status of survivors and whatever, but the next thing we heard was that the Edmonton plane had landed at Alert.

"When we heard this, we thought to ourselves, what the hell is going on here? We did know that a storm had been moving in, that things might not be good, but we never thought it would be so bad we couldn't get down.

"But when we got there, we did the same thing as Edmonton, I guess. We homed in on the site, dropped flares, tried to go down, and basically just scared the hell out of ourselves. This happened because we dropped a flare above the socked-in layer, then dove down through the clouds, thinking we might be able to see something under them when the flare came down that far. But the damned clouds went right to the ground and we almost had a head-on collision with our own flare, the flare we'd dropped up higher.

"But you couldn't see a thing — anywhere. And the area under us was so featureless anyway. We saw snow on snow and nothing more — even with the ramp open and everybody looking out, in the back and up front. Then by this time, we were getting short on gas but there was no room at Alert, so we flew to Thule. We knew that the guys from Edmonton were going to try again."

"We went back up, but it wasn't much better than before," Darby Darbyson explains, "and we kept flying and flying. But then we got some great news from the ground! We began to pick up a transmission from the crash site. Before their batteries down there gave out, we learned that there were fourteen survivors originally, but after a while knew that somebody had died. To save their power, a system was worked out so that the radio just had to be clicked: one click — ten alive; two clicks — twelve alive; and so on.

"The big boost to us was knowing that there were people alive down there, and we wanted to get in to help them. We tried everything we could. There were guys looking out back at the ramp, out the spotter's windows, up in the cockpit. At one point we dropped drift lights, but they were gone immediately, so we knew the winds were really bad. For a second, we thought we'd seen the site, but then we lost it and never saw it again. And we were never sure if it was the crash or just black rocks. By this time, we were completely burned out, so we went back to Alert."

While all this activity was going on in the skies above them, the crash survivors were in increasingly desperate straits. They did their best to adjust to the terrible circumstances: they coped with their injuries, tried to keep warm, radioed for help, counted heads, clustered together, prayed. At first, they thought they would be rescued quickly because most authorities knew they had to be somewhere close to Alert.

But as time passed, and the hours of blackness and suffering dragged on, spirits fell as surely as the temperature in this godforsaken place. And when the wrath of the winter gale eclipsed their world, survival itself was all-consuming. Two of the group, Bob Thomson and Susan Hillier, lay off by themselves, too badly injured to move or be moved. In time, they would be buried in snow. The others dragged themselves to the exposed, more or less intact hulk of the back of the plane, where they lay down, huddled together in a kind of metal cave. Their main commonality was the bitter cold.

"When we landed at Thule, we figured it was all over for us," Arnie Macauley continues. "We expected the Edmonton crew to get in, either in the air or on the ground. So we went to bed as soon as we got there, at a military hotel.

"After we had slept for about four hours, my brother called back to Alert to hear what was happening, and to ask if they needed us back in. They told us they did because the ground party had been forced back and the blizzard was still raging. But old Fred was going to go out again and they needed us to drop flares to guide them. So away we went again. That was when our ordeal really started.

"We piled into the Herc and did a real white-knuckle takeoff out of Thule. There was a crosswind, almost to the limit of the C-130. My brother had to pull off the line there to keep it on the runway, so we did basically a kind of three-engine takeoff. Finally he got the thing airborne, and scared everybody on board."

"The weather at Thule was getting worse, too," says Ron O'Reilly, "and we were maxed out on weight. We all knew that the runway there went towards a hill, and I remember it took an awfully long time before the wheels left the ground. Later, I was talking about our takeoff with one of the guys who had been up front. All he said was, 'Ron, you didn't want to be there.' I also was talking to one of the Americans there and he told me that ordinarily they would have closed the airport down, that they wouldn't have flown in that weather. They only kept it open for us so we could continue our search.

"When we got back over Alert, it was clearing near the ocean, but inland there was still a blizzard. Then we could see the lights of the tracked vehicles and had a fair idea about where they should go, so we started dropping flares to guide them. Every so often we would fly back over the crash site to see if we could see anything. We never could though."

Macauley continues: "We established radio contact with Fred and his guys and we guided them as best we could. But they couldn't see fifteen feet on the ground. Their compasses weren't working and they had ended up on sea ice earlier. We didn't want that to happen again, but guiding them was a hell of a lot of work. We did seven or eight hours of that and it was hard on everyone. We'd fly along, then the guys on the ground would get stuck, and a couple of times they went crashing over cliffs even when they had walkers out in front. When they got bogged down, we would go over to the crash site, home in on a beacon that was operating down there and see if we could see anything. We still couldn't, but we did get the ground party over the Sheridan River and onto flat ground and thought they would be our best bet at getting to the crash. They were perhaps two to four miles away.

"All this time, Fred was navigating by the altimeter on his watch, because nothing else worked. He knew the crash was at twelve hundred feet so he knew when the ground started to rise and he got to twelve hundred feet, he might be there.

"Then, one time, when we went back to where we thought the crash was, we were in the right place at the right time. We'd just dropped a flare, there was a slight clearing in the storm, and my God, we saw the tail, the tail of the bloody C-130! There was such a sense of relief for all of us on board. But then we came around again and never saw anything for another hour, and in all, we had been involved in this thing for about thirty hours at that point. Now, though, everyone knew something was going to happen."

"We didn't have enough headsets to go around," said Ron O'Reilly, "and because you can't hear anything in the back of a Herc, some of us were really pretty much in the dark as to what was going on. We were just sitting there waiting for the order to jump.

"During all this time, we were dropping flares, and the ramp at the back was open. Because the guys there were getting cold, we switched around every so often. I went back for a while along about then and had a chance to plug into an intercom outlet and hear what was going on. I remember Gerry Dominie was in the window, I was on the ramp, and Arnie was looking out as well, and Gerry saw something like a tail. Arnie saw something also and they asked me. I said I sort of saw a black object, but I wasn't sure whether it was a tail or not. Then we had another look and it was definitely a tail. That's when we got ready to go."

"We pretty much ignored the ground party at that point," Arnie Macauley explains. "They were still some distance away, and it didn't look as though they would get there soon, so I started briefing my guys on what we would be doing.

"We would go in in three different sticks [groups of jumpers]. The first stick was going to be six people with strictly medical gear, and they were going to go in and set up a triage — to treat the life-threatening injuries first, and so on. The second team was going to be responsible for the perimeter, to get the camp set up and retrieve the gear. The third team would stay on the airplane, drop all the gear and they would jump afterwards. The plan was okay, but then it went all to hell.

"Just as the first stick was about to go, the storm was moving out of there and we couldn't see a thing. But when we did see the tail again our own bloody contrails [exhaust] caused so much vapour in the air that everything would just fog over and cloud everything up again. At one point, we got off course when we thought we were at about a thousand feet, and we saw one of our own flares bouncing along the ground right under us.

"There was a lot going on in the front end, and the guys were working really hard to get the aircraft back over the spot again. Tensions were very high, lots of comments on the intercom, and everybody really frustrated.

"And of course, we all wanted to get on with it because people were dying down there, and the whole world was watching. This has been going on for well over a day now and nobody's in at the crash yet. Here we are, flying around, the ramp's open, it's forty below out there, and a hundred-knot wind is whipping around in the back of the plane. From the wheel wells aft, everything is frozen solid, we're scraping the ice off the windows, and the guys up front are cooking because we had to have as much heat as we could.

"Finally, we dropped another flare, saw the crash and decided this was it. Ordinarily, we never would have jumped in those conditions under two thousand feet, or in those winds. But we decided that the first six jumpers would go out, then a flare would be dropped right after them in the hope that it would come down somewhere near them and give them a bit of an idea of where the ground was. The flare burns for two minutes at two million candle power. Finally, we went out at a thousand feet.

"It was eerie coming down. The flare was an orange glow, and we could see it, but we could sense nothing else at all — other than an unbelievable blast of ice crystals. It took about forty-five seconds to come down, and at the last instant, I saw the tail of the crashed Herc right beside me and I thought I was going to hit it. We had drifted almost two miles coming down. We were really moving.

"One of our other jumpers, Bruce Best, was number two, and he came out of our plane behind me, but he hit the ground first. I saw him bounce, then the wind took his canopy and he was off like a shot, so then he collapsed his canopy right away. I remember hitting hard and the back of my head snapped into the ground with a thud. Then I felt myself getting picked up as the canopy started to take me away. It took a bit of struggle to control it."

At last, somebody had reached the crash site.

Macauley gathered his crew around him, made certain they secured all the equipment they carried, and then radioed up to his brother Marv to report that they were down and injury-free. Then the jumpers began stumbling, in pairs, through the snow, ice and blackness towards what remained of Boxtop 22.

"At this point, I don't think any of the survivors knew we were there," Macauley continues. "We swept through the wreckage, yelling as we went, but there was no response that we heard. Two guys went on the left, two more in the centre, and Ben House and I were on the right. The guys on the left found a couple of bodies along the way. As we went, we kept yelling to keep from getting lost. The storm was so wild that you could lose a guy fifteen feet away — and we had lights on our helmets. We had radios, but we didn't dare use them because they were pretty much useless. Three or four transmissions in that cold would kill them.

"I came up to the tail section and yelled in there, and for the first time, got an answer. The tail was wide open except for a liferaft that was bent up on one side a little, but the whole place was packed with snow. The snow was swirling around, and even with my headlamp I couldn't see much. I got down on my knees because there were a lot of sharp pieces of metal and junk, and for the first time I realized the floor was covered with people. You couldn't move without stepping on somebody. One guy, who I found out later was Mario Ellefsen, was at the feet of everyone, and I kind of fell into him, and he screamed. Later we found out he had a broken pelvis.

"Ben came in then, and we also got two more guys to come over. I was still not really talking to anyone yet but when one of the guys in there seemed a bit better than the others, I introduced myself. He said his name was Paul West. I told him I was Arnie Macauley and that we were all SAR Techs from Greenwood. He revived a bit, but all the others were stuporous. Nobody else made much sense and there was a lot of moaning.

"The first thing Paul tried to get across to us was that there were two others outside in the snow, and that we should try to find them. He thought the last contact with them was seven or eight hours before, but he wasn't even sure of that. He pointed outside and said they were 'over there somewhere, and they're buried in the snow.'

"Two guys stayed at the tail to do what they could, and Ben and I went out with Bruce Best and Derek Curtis to try to find the ones outside. As we went, we were kicking at stuff in the snow, and I remember pulling up about five parkas, because you couldn't tell if it was a person or not. Unfortunately, the survivors never found any of this stuff when they could have used it. This tells us something about the trauma of the crash....

"Anyway, the four of us did an entire sweep up one side and could not find anyone. But on the way back, Bruce and Derek found Thomson and Hillier covered in about three feet of snow. They were alive but were in bad shape — particularly Mr. Thomson.

"I remember being back at the tail of the plane again when the second stick — five guys — came down. As they got closer, the parachutes were silhouetted in the night from the flare they had just dropped. In a way, it was a beautiful sight, with all the ghostly looking orange crystals in the air. When the guys landed, they all grabbed their chutes pretty quickly, and then came over to us."

"As we came down I remember the yellow glow of the flare, and the ice crystals in the sky had this sparkling look," says Ron O'Reilly. "We could see the ground then, but the snow was still blowing. I could see the tracked vehicles and it looked as though they would arrive at the crash site as soon as us, but it was still a while. As we got closer to the ground, we could see dark objects and white objects, so I decided to stay away from the dark objects because they were likely rocks.

"Once you were on the ground, it was a blizzard, and the only things you could see were the strobe lights of the other guys. I remember cutting one of my risers so I wouldn't be dragged away in the wind, and then grabbing my chute right away. As I was doing so, I thought that if I couldn't find the crash site, at least this would be some shelter. Even though we were all together, you could be in a total whiteout in two minutes. I think we all thought the chutes might be needed if we got lost.

"By the time we had our chutes looked after, we were ready to start walking to where we thought the crash was. I remember coming up to the tail, and it was wide open. It was then that Arnie suggested we put the parachutes over the end as a bit of wind break. That helped some."

"The last three guys didn't get to jump," Arnie Macauley explains. "They did one more pass and threw the equipment out, but because they were on bingo fuel they had to get to Alert and land right away. Unfortunately, the equipment they dropped was all lost — $280,000 worth of it. I know because I had to do the complete inventory later. They dropped it in the right place, but the winds were so strong, they took it all. We did see a couple of big bundles go by, but they went as fast as a horse could gallop. We had no way of stopping it.

"The situation in the tail of the plane was really bad. I knew those people had lain down for the last time. None of them could walk; not even Paul West. They were frozen to the metal floor with a combination of sweat at first and condensation, then urine. If we had not been able to get there when we did, I know that where they were was where they would have been found ...

"We had a terrible time trying to break them free from the metal. Some we just took out by cutting their clothes. They were in such a hell of a mess, but we had to worry about the hypothermia as well as the various injuries. By this time we had found another body outside, and pilot John Couch as well, who was lying beside Mario. We removed the body at that point. Meanwhile, some of the other guys were working with Sue Hillier and Bob Thomson outside."

After the Edmonton plane had reached Alert earlier on, the crew was fed and given places to sleep. A bit more room was made on the tarmac for the second Herc, when the shortage of fuel made it essential that they come in also. But the amount of rest anyone got through all the hours of turmoil was almost negligible.

"I was in a bed next to a phone," recalls Darby Darbyson. "I don't think I'd even closed my eyes when it started ringing. I grabbed it of course, and somebody told me the Greenwood guys were on the ground and needed help.

"We were out of there — and three of the Greenwood SAR Techs who didn't jump earlier, Keith McKellar, Gerry Dominie and Marc Lessard, climbed into our Herc and we took off. But the weather was still terrible over the crash.

"We jumped from about eight hundred feet, and we couldn't see a thing. Jim Brown went out first, then myself and

Shawn MacDiarmid came out behind me. I saw Jim hit the
ground, or what I thought was the ground, and I saw Shawn
hit. I hit, and even though I had a good landing, I blew into
Jim, chute and all.

"When we got organized, we didn't know where we were,
and about that time we started to wonder what we'd gotten
ourselves into. We later found out we were about two miles
from the crash site. It was in the middle of a blizzard, dark, and
you could see nothing at all. So we got on the radio to the
aircraft and asked them to have the guys at the crash fire off a
flare to give us direction, because not one of us knew where to
go, nor had any one of us seen the crash as we came down.

"So we stood in a circle, looking out, like a bunch of muskox,
but we saw the flare off in the distance. In order to keep from
getting lost, we decided to leapfrog towards it. Two guys would
walk a short way, then two more would walk to them and go a
bit beyond. Then two more would come up and so on. We kept
doing that, lining each pair up, and yelling back and forth all the
time to keep from getting lost. Every so often, we'd ask for
another flare to keep us in the right direction. We always had to
talk to the plane and they talked to Arnie, because there was a
hill between us and the crash site.

"Then as we started getting closer, we could see gouges in
the snow and pieces of wreckage. After we'd been walking for
about two hours, and some of the guys were hurt doing the
jump, we were pretty happy to be getting close to where there
were people. Walking across the tundra after being lost was not a
lot of fun. We were lucky there wasn't another search for us.
This was my first operational jump, and I told myself I would
never do another one like it. The next time, I would know
where I was jumping, and at least what I was getting into. We
pushed it and were lucky.

"We came to a ridge line that was between a hundred and as
much as two hundred feet high, which the aircraft had hit.
Then we walked down a slope, into a bowl and came to the site.
There was a mass of metal everywhere, but apart from the tail,

it was hard to tell that it had been an airplane. The whole scene was so strange. There was no light other than the headlamps of the SAR Techs who were there, and occasionally the light from a flare up above that our Herc was dropping to guide the ground party.

"The first guy I saw was Ron O'Reilly, and I remember asking him if there was anyone still alive — the place looked so bad. He said, 'Oh, yes there is. Glad you guys made it okay.' So were we."

For the SAR Techs at the scene, the next hours began to run together. Those I interviewed for this book remember some things in vivid detail, but other matters, faces, and even a few of their efforts have been forgotten. For one thing, they were all desperately tired, but without exception kept going long after human beings are supposed to give out. Their actions in that frozen hell were exemplary. Had they not been there, not a single person on Boxtop 22 would have come out alive. Yet every man who risked his life to get to the crash site downplayed what he did, deflected the credit, scoffed at praise, and in various ways said simply: "It was my job."

For so long in the operation, things had gone wrong. The storm never really abated in all the time the rescue teams were trying to get on scene. The ground parties kept getting lost, and almost died in their journey. The last group of SAR Techs who jumped could easily have perished on the trackless tundra. The equipment blew away almost as soon as it left the planes. The litany of problems seemed endless, but then — mercifully — it did end.

"They [the problems] began to end when a couple of my guys, Jean Tremblay and Rob Walker, found a toboggan jammed into some boulders somewhere," recalls Arnie Macauley. "They brought it in, took a tent out of it and were beginning to set it up, just as the last group of jumpers came over the hill. The tent was a six-man SAR tent, about six feet wide and ten long, and there was also a lantern. They set the tent up, got the light in there, and finally we had some place to put Hillier and

Thomson, to get them some protection. At about this time, Fred Ritchie and the two tracked vehicles from Alert arrived.

"We had been at the site for two hours and forty-five minutes when the bloody ground party pulled over the horizon. I know when I saw old Fred, I was never so happy to see anyone in my life. They had more tents, cases of pop, chocolate bars, coleman stoves, all the things Base Alert had given them. We set up more tents, got some people melting snow for water, started to warm up our IVs because they were frozen solid, and began moving people inside."

"The tail section was an unbelievable scene," Darby Darbyson says, with a perceptible shudder. "The parachutes were over the opening when I went there, and then inside, there was another chute over the people. It was hard to distinguish where they were, and you didn't want to step on people. I'll never forget the moaning. It was like walking into a meat freezer. Then everyone would be absolutely silent.

"I went to one guy, Mario Ellefsen as I later found out, and started to feel around to see what I could do for him. He was in severe pain, and his clothes were frozen to the ramp. He said his back hurt, and this was because his pelvis was broken. We had to try to figure out how to get him loose without hurting him any more than necessary. Finally we shot him up with morphine, cut his clothes off, put him into a sleeping bag, and carried him to one of the tracked vehicles. Ben House started an IV in him and we got him into MAST pants [anti-shock trousers] to stabilize his fractures. At least now, his broken bones weren't grinding on one another. He was conscious all the time."

"Once we got one or two out of the tail, we had a bit more room in there," Arnie Macauley continues. "But before we were able to give them morphine, we had to be able to monitor them because they were in such a sorry state. Morphine is a respiratory depressant, so if you give it to somebody who is too weak, you could stop them from breathing, and kill them. That's why we had to be so careful. And of course, everyone in the tail had been drenched in the damned diesel fuel, and that, along with the sweat and condensation and urine, made it so bad for them all. That was before you even considered their broken bones and burns."

"I remember working on one guy who was in bad shape," Ron O'Reilly says. "He told me he had to pee in the worst way. I told him to go ahead, that we were going to cut his clothes off anyway. I guess that okay wasn't the best, because right afterwards, he relaxed and was right out of it. Then he didn't respond anymore. I knew he likely had a fractured skull, but I didn't know whether it or hypothermia was the bigger problem. Anyway, we got his clothes off, I did a rectal temperature check to see what his core temperature was, and we got him into a sleeping bag and started an IV.

"Working in a tracked vehicle was difficult because we were in such close quarters. I recall bumping into the doc's [Doctor Wilma de Groot, a crash survivor] broken ankle, and she wasn't too happy. But when I gave her some morphine, she was happy.

"And we were really getting burned out by this time. I'm not sure of the number of hours, but it seemed like a couple of days without sleep. When you were outside, you were in the cold, but after working in the warmth of the tracked vehicles for a while, the adrenaline rush began wearing off and you felt so sleepy. I remember trying to get an IV into one person, but I was falling asleep and I couldn't see the vein. I got someone else to do the stick for me and I got out for a few minutes in the cold to wake up."

While his men were doing their best to save the lives of those they worked on, Arnie Macauley was on the radio, talking to the base surgeon from Edmonton, who was now at Alert. Macauley knew that soon a Twin Huey helicopter, also from Edmonton but being partly assembled at Alert, would be in for the survivors, and he wanted to do all he could to prepare the personnel at the northern base for what they could expect. He knew too, that a field hospital was ready there for them. Finally, the helicopter arrived.

"We knew the Twin Huey could only take four stretchers at a

time, so we picked the most serious for the first flight out," Macauley explains. "I think the next was two stretcher cases and three survivors who were ambulatory, and so on. Anyway, we got all the injured out in three lifts. Six SAR Techs had gone with them, and then the Huey broke down.

"Fortunately, it didn't cause a great problem because we had been told two American Pavehawks [helicopters] from Elmendorf [in Alaska] had been taken to Thule, and they would be in to help us bring everyone else out. Well, the Pavehawks arrived okay, but because of their size, when they landed, their rotor wash smashed down all our tents and broke them up. We were damned lucky we didn't need them anymore.

"But at the very end, there was another problem. I wanted to send everyone who was left out on the last flight — including the bodies of the five victims. Well, the American pilots didn't want to take the bodies, so I talked to somebody higher up in Alert. Alert talked to the pilots, and the bodies were taken."

And so the saga in the far north came to a conclusion. The exhausted SAR Techs, navigators, pilots, flight engineers, loadmasters and so many others could relax at last. The men who flew the helicopter from Trenton to Eureka on Ellesmere Island could enter the realm of legend — but that is another story.

And now there are two memorials at Alert. Each is a reminder of something terrible that happened there, first in 1950 and again in 1991. The stone cairns stand together, on the windswept wilderness at the top of the world.

15

Death in the Snow

When the police checked the truck, the owners were nowhere around. Nor had they been for some time. In fact, the vehicle was the only indication that they had passed that way at all. Fresh snow had long since obliterated both footprints and ski tracks, and the note in the cab was several days old.

Yet Robert Kovacs, 33, was a careful hiker. So was his 34-year-old wife Jennie. They knew the bush, they knew the terrain, and they understood and respected the vagaries of weather. Their letter on the truck seat explained where they intended to hike, the trails they would use and the date they hoped to return. When the return time passed with no sign of the pair, the RCMP was informed. The Mounties began a ground search, but when they found no trace of the missing pair, they alerted the Rescue Co-Ordination Centre in Victoria. The hikers were presumably still high up in the rugged Coast Mountains, southeast of the small community of Bella Coola, B.C.

The first of two Search and Rescue Labrador helicopters from

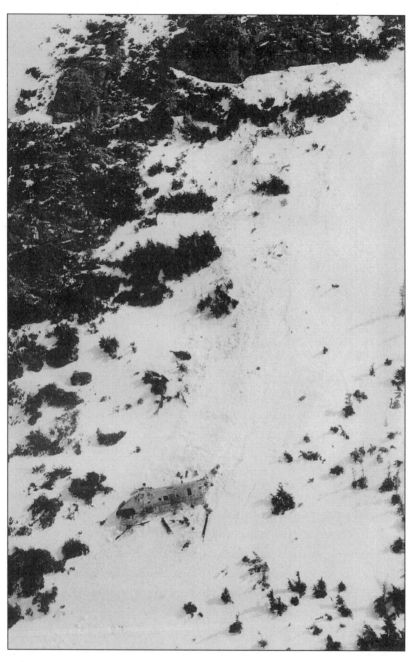

The crash site of Rescue 311. The helicopter hit the British Columbia mountainside, at the top of the picture, then rolled several times before coming to rest in wreckage and flames. (Canadian Forces photo by Ben Lafrance)

Comox tasked to the mission arrived on scene during the morning of April 29, 1992. The second came in a day later, but already Robert and Jennie were a week overdue. By this time, family and friends were starting to fear the worst.

While the mountains in the Bella Coola area of British Columbia are undeniably beautiful, they are wild, lonely, and remote. By car, the town itself is over six hundred miles from Vancouver, over roads that are often gravel. Tweedsmuir Park is nearby, and the search for the Kovacs was conducted there. It was like looking for one rock on the surface of Mars.

"It took some time to get in by helicopter," recalls Don Harper, a SAR Tech with 442 Squadron at Comox. "I was on the second to arrive, and we knew the guys ahead of us had found nothing."

Both helicopters operated out of the Bella Coola airport, while their crews were billeted at a motel in the town. The military were assisted in the search by local residents who volunteered because they knew the area. This group included police officers, park employees and hikers. Some continued the ground search, while others worked as spotters in the air. The choppers covered different segments of the park.

"We dropped off some of the guys who would be on the ground," Harper continues. "They were flown to particular places and then we took off and searched farther up some of the valleys. The job was tiring and frustrating because there was no sign of anyone, but you can never give up. I was on 312."

Don Harper's remark identifies the helicopter he rode. All aircraft in the Canadian military are numbered in this way. In Harper's case, the big yellow Labrador chopper was tagged "Rescue 312." Its counterpart in the operation, Rescue 311, was identical in every way. Al Burley rode in it.

Burley was one of two flight engineers on the second aircraft. The other military personnel on board were Greg Lewis, Ron Langevin, and Al Banky. The two pilots were Joel Clarkson and Gabriel Ringuette. All were experienced in rescue work. At the end of the day, they would pick up the ground party dropped off

Rescue 311, the ill-fated Labrador helicopter on the dock at Tofino, British Columbia, shortly before a crash near Bella Coola. (Canadian Forces photo)

Flight engineer Al Burley, left, suffered severe injuries in the crash of the Labrador helicopter, Rescue 311. Don Harper, right, was one of the first SAR Techs to reach the downed plane.

in the morning by 312. Both helicopters would return to Bella Coola for fuel.

"For the most part, the weather on the second day of the search was good," Al Burley remembers. "There were a few clouds, though, and later the weather began to close in. We decided to pick up the guys on the ground and get out of there. There was still no trace of the Kovacs."

"It was not snowing, but it was close to it," said Don Harper. "We were getting low on fuel, and in view of the way the weather was looking we told 311 we were going back to base. There was still more daylight left, but it was decided that we would pack up for the day."

Rescue 312 flew south by southwest down the Bella Coola River towards town. The first flakes of snow were in the air as they reached the airport.

"We gassed up as soon as we got in," Harper continues, "and then we tied up the blades and had the covers on. We expected 311 to come in at any minute. However, it was not to be I guess...

"We were down for about forty-five minutes or so when RCC called. They told us they were getting an ELT hit in the search area, and asked when we'd had our last transmission from 311."

The message stunned those who heard it. It also galvanized them into an immediate response. "We couldn't believe it," said Don Harper. "We had just talked to those guys, and everything was okay. At first we figured if the ELT was theirs, it had gone off accidentally or something, but we got ready to go back up there in a hell of a hurry anyway."

In no time, Rescue 312 was prepped and ready to go. The engines were started and the big propellers fore and aft rotated faster and faster. Then, less than fifteen minutes after the RCC call, the chopper lifted off the tarmac and headed into the hills. On board was a group of men feeling apprehension and dread. None knew what to expect.

Nor had those whom they sought.

Only an hour earlier, Rescue 311 was operating normally. It

had done a final sweep over some unchecked bush, and then, after contacting the searchers on the ground, prepared to drop down for them. At first, the pickup seemed routine.

"The guys were waiting for us as we approached," explains Al Burley. "The pickup area was not too difficult for a hoist, even though it was around the five-thousand-foot level. It was a place where there were no trees in the way."

There were four men waiting on the ground: two civilians who were part of the Provincial Emergency Programme (PEP) team, and two SAR Techs. They all had cross country skis and poles, all of which would be taken on board and stowed for the resumption of the search in the morning. The PEP members, nurse Andy Schmidt and mountie Roger Harris, were hoisted first.

"We were about thirty feet from the ground," Burley goes on. "After the civilians were on board, Phil Young came up with an armload of skis and poles. Phil was one of the SAR Techs. The other one was Tony Isaacs who was coming up last."

But Isaacs did not get his turn.

Suddenly, with no warning whatsoever, one of the helicopter's engines quit.

Instantly, the big machine lurched to one side and dropped.

In the cockpit, Major Joel Clarkson, who was flying at the time, manoeuvred to his right, to the downslope side, desperately fighting for air in a futile attempt to keep the ship up.

"I remember Phil coming in the door and handing somebody some skis," Al Burley continues, "and then the next second, Major Clarkson's voice in my headset. I'm not sure of his exact words, but I think he said, 'Holy Jesus, we've lost an engine!'

"Then there was a second or so of silence, and we all thought, 'You've done what?' It was so unbelievable. I knew the Lab could fly on one engine, but there is a lag time before the single one resumes power.

"Major Clarkson did all he could, but there just wasn't time. I don't think we had a chance, really.

"As we slid to the right, I remember that Al Banky [a SAR Tech] was sitting on the sill inside the open door of the aircraft.

Greg Lewis [the second flight engineer on board] and I managed to grab his harness and push him into the companionway leading to the cockpit."

Al Banky's memory of the moment is equally vivid. He described it in the Winter 1993 issue of *Airforce* magazine: "I will never forget the sound of the engine winding down; the pilots, Major Joel Clarkson and Captain Gab Ringuette, used all their skills to keep the helicopter in the air.... As the helicopter started its sidewards roll down the mountainside, Mcpls Al Burley and Greg Lewis, our flight engineers, reached forward and pulled me back from the open door from which I had been hoisting. It always seems strange how the military can train someone to override their own survival instincts in favour of helping those for whom they are responsible."

"We had no sooner gotten Al away from the door," Burley continues, "than I fell on my rear end, back from the door and the plane hit the snow. But that's when all hell broke loose.

"The initial impact hit the left-hand sponson, the gas tank, and that cart-wheeled us to the right side and down the mountain. We were on monkey harnesses [safety harnesses] tethered to a line hooked to the side of the aircraft. The harness is attached at the centre of your back so your arms and legs are free for working and movement.

"As the plane kept rolling over, the fact that I was hooked to the line made me feel like one of those balls attached by an elastic to a paddle that a kid plays with. Only I was the ball and I felt myself being thrown all over the place and then coming up short when the line came tight. As we were coming down, I'd be tossed headfirst into something, then the aircraft would roll again, and I would be yanked back against the radio rack or whatever. Then we would flip another time and I was on the ceiling, then on the floor and so on. The other guys were flying around the same way."

Outside, and by now some distance uphill, Tony Isaacs watched in abject horror as the helicopter he had been about to board rolled over and over, tearing itself apart in the mad, terrible plunge down the mountain. Sounds of breaking steel, aluminum and glass, coupled at first with the roar of the engine, echoed and re-echoed against the canyon walls. Chunks of wildly spinning rotor blades flew through the air, as the trail of debris went on and on and on.

Isaacs was sure no one in the craft would survive.

And his fears threatened to become real.

Instinctively, he lunged through the snow, downhill, in the direction the helicopter had gone. If there were survivors he had to help.

Then tragically, only a few steps lower, he came upon the lifeless body of his friend Phil Young, the last man up the hoist, lying amid the broken red and black and yellow pieces of the doomed aircraft.

In the helicopter itself, the turmoil continued.

"We seemed to roll forever, eight or nine times," Al Burley says. "Everything was a jumble. I remember in one of the rolls, my right shoulder popped — dislocated — and I recall thinking, 'That is more than a little bruise. This is going to hurt.' Then I was thrown on that shoulder again and it broke. I blacked out with the pain. When I came to, I was lying on the floor feeling groggy. I remember looking up at that point and seeing one of the civilian searchers standing in front of me, his forehead split open and part of his flesh hanging down."

"I remember flashes of green and grey and white as we tumbled down the mountainside," Burley continues. "Then, when we finally came to a stop, there was black smoke coming in the door."

Farther back inside the fuselage, civilian nurse Andy Schmidt attempted to get his bearings and later admitted, in an interview with the *Vancouver Sun* on May 2, 1992, that "we were afraid the whole thing was going to go up in a ball of flame." At the time of these thoughts, Schmidt was unaware of his two crushed vertebrae, of the bruises all over his body, and of the deep facial and scalp cuts he had suffered.

Al Burley recalls the point when the tumbling stopped. "On

the last roll, Greg Lewis was thrown partway through the hatch, but when the aircraft stopped, it came to rest across his legs. And he was still in his harness. Somebody was yelling, 'Undo his harness, we're on fire!'

"I still had my own harness on. It is designed to release quickly, but I couldn't get at it. I couldn't reach around behind my back to do it because my right arm was useless and was just hanging there hurting like hell. I finally got unhooked with my left hand.

"By now there was a lot of smoke, and we're on fire and everything is all confused, and Greg is still pinned under the plane. I remember unhooking Greg's harness, and then being out in the snow."

Some of the crewmen were out before Burley; one was Ron Langevin, and another was Al Banky. Banky would later describe what he saw: "I flipped myself outside through one of the emergency exits and ended up on the downhill side of the wreck with Ron Langevin. We walked around the nose of the plane and for the first time began to realize and appreciate the seriousness of what had just occurred. Away up above were the remains of the fuel tank we'd lost. Still higher were chunks of rotor blades, and down lower as well. There were pieces of junk everywhere.

"Flames were jumping from the overturned right fuel tank, which was on the upslope side. At that point, Greg Lewis was trapped under the helicopter and the flames were coming closer to him. Those of us who could walk stood against the uphill side of the wreck and tried to push it off him. I remember that Ron was one of these, even though he had a dislocated shoulder.

"At this point, the crew split into two. I'm not sure exactly who did what, but those involved in rescuing Greg stayed in the cloud of smoke and flames and dug and pried until they managed to pull him out. Those not involved in freeing Greg worked at smothering the fire. The contents of a fire extinguisher were emptied onto the flames; the fire died quickly and just as quickly flashed up again. Broken pieces of windscreen were used to scoop up snow and pile it on the flames until the fire was finally out."

Al Burley remembers lying in the snow as the fire raged. "Several of the guys were on their hands and knees fighting it," he says. "Major Clarkson, Gabby Ringuette, Al Banky, Ronnie … They were scooping snow with anything they could, with their hands…."

By that time, Tony Isaacs had worked his way down the mountain to the wreck. He had been spotted a minute or two earlier by Banky and Langevin. Banky relates the story: "As we looked up the slope, Tony stood on the ledge above which we had been hovering. The look on his face was one of amazement, not amazement at what had just happened, but amazement that there were people actually clambering out of a helicopter that had just rolled five hundred feet down the side of a mountain in a ball of flames."

"From the time the CO said we'd lost an engine, to the point when the whole thing was over, was only fifteen seconds, twenty at most," says Al Burley, "but from the time we hit to the time we stopped and I passed out seemed like three or four minutes. We had been at thirty- to thirty-five-foot hover with a weight of 17,000 pounds or so, and the Lab fell like a rock. I know it was the longest fifteen seconds of my life.

"Then I remember Tony and some of the guys who were not too badly off grabbing our first aid equipment and doing what they could. The civilian whose scalp was ripped was bandaged and the next thing I knew Ron and Tony were wrapping me to keep me warm. I was shivering pretty badly and my shoulder hurt so much I wanted to pass out again, but otherwise I was okay."

As soon as the fire around the plane was out and the injured removed from it, a couple of the SAR Techs began putting up a tent on the snow pack a short distance to the side. By the time it was erected, Andy Schmidt, the civilian nurse, felt himself getting woozy. "I was pumped so full of adrenalin that helping others was no problem at first," he recalled. "All of a sudden I just seized up. It was incredible that I could be moving one minute and then feel myself going the next." He had to be dragged into the tent.

Somebody handed Al Burley an ELT and told him to hold it. "I remember the sound of it drove me nuts," he remembers, "but it sure worked. It seemed that in no time we could hear the sound of the other chopper. As we waited, Ronnie Langevin was doing a head count. I remember hearing him yelling for Phil Young when he realized we were a man short. But then Tony Isaacs went over and spoke to him, and he didn't call anymore...."

In the meantime, Rescue 312 was climbing up the canyon, following the ever-stronger ELT signal from the sister ship. Soon after, they were able to establish radio contact with the ground, and in doing so confirmed their worst fears.

"Up until that point, we were hoping they had had to set down because of the weather," says Don Harper, who was on 312. "But that was not the case, unfortunately. Ron Langevin's voice came on and I remember him saying, 'We've crashed. We've crashed. We've crashed.' We got the location from him, and then came around a mountain ridge and saw their smoke and a flare. But while we could see them, we had to dump fuel in order to get up to them.

"As soon as we knew they had crashed, one of our pilots asked about the extent of injuries, if there were any, and so on. We then heard Ronnie say they had one black [one person dead] and several who were injured, but we couldn't dwell on that. We had to suck back and reload for a little bit, but it didn't take much time for us to click in and start the process of what we had to do to get them out. From then on, we did what our training demanded."

The second chopper experienced considerable difficulty getting high enough up the mountain to effect the rescue. Because the aircraft had just been refuelled, it was quite heavy, but as it turned out, several pieces of non-essential equipment had to be jettisoned through the open rear ramp, along with the excess fuel that was also dumped.

Both 312 pilots, in tandem with the flight engineers on board, did a praiseworthy job of getting to the crash. Gradually however, they succeeded in working their way up the hill to a place where they felt it would be safe to hover.

"The pilots were not sure of the winds, which are always

The wreckage of Rescue 311 lies on a British Columbia mountainside. The photo was taken after the fire had been put out, and after the dead and injured were removed.
(Canadian Forces photo by Ben Lafrance)

tricky in the mountains," continues Harper, "and they didn't want our own prop wash to make things worse on the ground. Finally we got a reference though and Paul Beattie and I were hoisted down from about sixty feet.

"We went down into what was basically a forty-five-degree snowbank and we had to work to get up from there. This would have been 100 to 150 yards below the crash, and the snow was chest-deep. I remember being winded by the time I reached the wreck, even though I was on max adrenalin. Then seeing the crash close up was a shock, because you knew all the guys who had been in it. The fact that I could have been one of them didn't sink in until later.

"Paul was hoisted down first and he was up at the scene first. By the time I got there, the tent was set up and Greg Lewis had been taken into it along with one or two of the others. I went right to the tent to help — and that's where I was when I learned who didn't make it. We had to keep going though. Al Banky, Tony and the others had already set up the triage [system of priorities] and it was pretty well decided who to look after first.

"By this time, the helicopter had gotten up closer to the scene so we began bringing the injured out for hoisting. Other than Tony, everyone came up in a Stokes litter. Paul directed from the ground, and the two RCMP guys who came out with us were a great help. We had a real plane load getting out of there though. There were sixteen of us on board; we were terribly crowded, and the weather was getting worse. We knew we could never get back a second time. As it was, Phil's body had to be left behind because our priority was with the living. Because the weather stayed bad, his body wasn't removed for four days.

"On the way down to Bella Coola we were stumbling over one another. I remember just being able to get one IV going. There were five stretcher cases — three in the back and two up closer to the front. One guy was lying in a sled on the floor.

"We landed at the airport first, but then because there were so many who needed medical help, it was decided that we should fly right to the hospital. Luckily there was a schoolyard close by and we landed there. By this time the bingo lights [warning of low fuel] were on and it was pretty close. Later we had to have fuel trucked to the schoolyard so we could take off. I remember that it was almost dark and drizzling as we took the guys into the hospital. Up in the rocks at the crash site it was snowing."

Those who were injured on Rescue 311 were treated at Bella

Coola, and in some instances flown to Vancouver for more specialized medical treatment. All recovered from the ordeal of the crash, but Al Burley's return to work came last. When his shoulder shattered, the impact drove the end of the bone into nerve bundles under his right armpit. For a time, his right arm and hand were immobile, and even today the feeling in that hand is not as it once was. Yet, following two years of operations, painful therapy, exercise, and willing himself to be well, he returned to the job he loves. Today he still works in Search and Rescue — on the Hercules aircraft.

*   *   *   *   *

Several months after the crash of Rescue 311, several SAR Techs, and others who knew Phil Young, erected a memorial to him, high on the mountainside where he gave his life to help others.

The objects of the search — the Kovacses — also died in the British Columbia mountains. Their bodies were located long afterwards, still roped together, having probably died in an avalanche.

16

That Others May Live

The *Paula and Jordan* is at the bottom of the Atlantic Ocean now, sixty miles east of Cape Race, Newfoundland. The forty-two-foot green-and-white fishing boat sank in a vicious storm on June 18, 1992, but her crew of four was saved in one of the most difficult and terrifying rescues imaginable. In fact, the rescuers themselves are lucky to be alive.

Three days before his boat sank, 30-year-old Bill Dawe said goodbye to his wife Shellie, eased the *Paula and Jordan* away from the dock at St. John's, and headed for the open sea. On board with him were his father, also named Bill, his brother Randy, and his nephew Jimmy Oakley. They were going to catch flounder.

The boat in which they rode was twenty-one years old, but Bill Dawe had purchased it only eight months before. He knew the vessel was trustworthy, and he was proud to take it to sea. This would be his first major trip as its owner.

It would also be Jimmy Oakley's first trip of this kind. The

19-year-old had not been to sea before. He was happy to be there, happy to be with his grandfather and uncles. Happy to be of help. Happy to be needed.

The first part of the trip was without incident. The weather was reasonably good, the seas were moderate, and the *Paula and Jordan* made good time. On the second day, however, and then into the third, a low-pressure area blanketed the fishing grounds. The ocean swells grew higher, the winds picked up, and the grey skies brought relentless rain.

"Everything got worse," Bill Dawe explains. "The seas got rougher, and we started taking on a lot of water. We had to pump the boat out more or less continuously, but then we started to lose the battle. We lost all track of time, and I knew we were in real trouble. Finally, I put out a mayday."

On the morning of the third day, Environment Canada issued a gale warning for Newfoundland coastal waters. Visibility was rated poor and winds in excess of thirty-five knots were expected. Mariners were advised to take note. But all this was too late for the crew of the *Paula and Jordan*.

Dawe tried to keep his vessel into the wind, hoping it could ride out the ocean rollers. And for a while, it did. The craft would seem almost motionless at times, but a few seconds later it would ride the crest of a wave, then plunge deep into the trough that followed. When it went down into the back of a monstrous swell, it took on water. When it was high on a crest, the northeast winds shrieked across the deck, tore at the bow, and tossed the boat like a bauble. At such times, the skipper knew that if he couldn't keep his *Paula and Jordan* head-to, she would probably be swamped and roll over. Holding on was torture. Waiting for help was forever.

But the SOS had been heard.

"We were down off the south coast of Newfoundland on a training flight," says SAR Tech Bill Barber. "RCC Halifax called and told us there was a fishing vessel with four souls on board sinking fifty or sixty miles off Cape Race. We were also informed that the people on the boat were about to go into a liferaft.

"Because we didn't have enough gas to get out to them, do the mission and get back, we topped off at St. John's and headed out. It was a hot refuel [one in which the aircraft engines are running while gas is being pumped] because of the urgency of the call. The weather had been okay when we left Gander earlier on, but at St. John's it was not as good and as we got a few miles out over the ocean, it got worse — a lot worse. By the time we found the boat, the weather was absolutely terrible. The winds were strong, the ceiling was quite low and the waves were at least thirty feet in height. The helicopter was bouncing around all over the place.

Kelly Jamieson, above, was the pilot of a Labrador helicopter during the nerve-wracking rescue of four fishermen in the Atlantic storm.
Bill Barber, right, was a SAR Tech on the same mission.

"About the only thing we did not have to worry about that day was icing," explains Major Kelly Jamieson, the aircraft commander. "The weather was fairly warm, but the visibility up higher was nonexistent, so we stayed down at three hundred feet or so. It wasn't a horrendous distance out, but that didn't matter because nobody was going to swim to shore. We knew we had to get to them as quickly as we could."

"We were pretty happy when we saw the chopper," laughs Bill Dawe. "I don't think we could have held on much longer. The sea was just so bad, I knew the boat would sink. We just didn't want it to sink with us on it. And the waves were thirty feet high, later on forty or more."

"It was the worst sea I can remember," Bill Barber admits, "and by the time we saw that boat, we knew we had our work cut out for us."

As soon as they were over the foundering *Paula and Jordan*, Jamieson and his co-pilot Marty Zimmer tried to decide how to position the helicopter to effect the rescue. "The little boat was really getting walloped," Jamieson says. "It was riding so low in the water, we were afraid it was going to go down before we could do anything. The strange thing was, there were five or six other boats around, but the seas were too high for them to help. Here they were, watching, even taking pictures like interested bystanders, waiting to see what we were going to do.

"There are problems with little boats. It's hard to get a reference on them at any time, it's even worse in rough seas because of the vertical motion, the pitch and roll, and boats that have lost or can't do much to control their steering are harder still. Anyway, the two SAR Techs we had on the chopper were the best in the business, and they were ready to go down on the hoist."

While all this was happening out on the Atlantic, Shellie Dawe had been watching the weather and thinking about Bill and the others on the *Paula and Jordan*. "They were always on my mind," she says, "and because the weather was so terrible, I knew they would be having a bad day. I just didn't know then how bad."

Fortunately, Shellie did not know of a conversation her mother-in-law had had with Bill's sister Jeannie early that morning.

Kathleen Dawe had slept fitfully. She tossed and turned all

night, and finally, around 5:00 A.M. awoke from a terrible nightmare, only to find that the nightmare would not go away. She was filled with profound fear, a dread of impending disaster. Finally, unable to concentrate on anything else, and knowing she could not sleep, Mrs. Dawe got up and brewed a cup of tea. She was sitting at the kitchen table when Jeannie arrived home from work an hour later.

"Mom, what are you doing up so early?" Jeannie asked.

"Oh, I'm just having a cup of tea; I couldn't sleep," Mrs. Dawe told her daughter. Then she added, "The boys are in trouble. They're having trouble. There's trouble on that boat. I *know*."

Jeannie put the matter out of her mind — even though her mother's premonition was, at that moment, becoming real.

"I came up close to the boat," Major Jamieson explained, "and finally got a reference for the hoist. I believe Tom Taylor was the SAR Tech who went down first. Then Bill Barber was hoisted down and I was starting to think that this might not be too bad after all. But I was wrong. Boy, was I wrong."

As soon as the two SAR Techs were on the *Paula and Jordan*, they began preparing the crew for the hoisting. First to go would be 58-year-old Bill Dawe, Sr. Barber would take him up.

"I put the horsecollar on him," explains Barber, "and Tom held the guideline so the hoist wouldn't swing. We signalled Kevin Morawski, our flight engineer, and he started the hoist. But just as the cable began to tighten, the boat slid down off a huge wave."

The action was unexpected, and it came at the wrong time. At precisely the same moment, Kelly Jamieson lost sight of the boat, and had to back off to regain his reference. Suddenly, the helicopter and the *Paula and Jordan* were much farther from each other, yet Barber and Dawe were hooked on the cable that linked the two. Like an elastic band stretched too far, the effect was immediate.

The steel cable tightened, the men on the end of it were jerked off their feet, catapulted across the deck, and slammed into a tubular metal railing at the back of the boat. They were then flipped high into the air, only to crash down on the top of the railing, after which they fell onto the deck. The cable to the chopper, the lifeline to safety, had snapped.

"Everything took place so fast, at first I couldn't figure out what happened," Bill Barber recalls. "One minute I was giving the thumbs-up to Kevin. The next, Mr. Dawe and I were lying on the deck and my partner was looking at us with a strange look on his face.

"But as soon as I realized what was wrong, I remember turning to Tom and saying, 'We are not getting off this boat today. We're going to have to go into the liferaft and take our chances.'" Barber now admits that he was sure that they would all die. The seas were wild, and the main way out was gone. But then, in an almost instantaneous reaction, he grabbed his radio and told the men up above to get another chopper — fast!

"Bill Barber was amazing, even after what happened to him," Kelly Jamieson says. "We had barely realized something was wrong, when he was telling us how to fix it. So Marty picked up the HF and ordered another chopper. Luckily, Gander had one available."

But the second helicopter was not on standby; no-one was on hand, ready to jump into it and go. Quickly, however, a front-end crew was rounded up and the machine took off. No SAR Techs were on board.

"The Lab has a centre hoist, down through the floor of the plane," Kelly Jamieson explains. "However, hoisting from there is very difficult. If you're doing the flying, you're basically doing it blind. You can't see what's below you. You have to rely on others for your every move. However, Kevin Morawski was working his head off in the back, getting ready. The centre hoist was all we had, so we had to try it."

In order to give Jamieson some reference, because he had to be directly over the *Paula and Jordan*, Morawski dropped smoke cannisters into the water near the boat. They were intended as markers for the pilots.

"The smoke was a help," says Jamieson, "but the cannisters

kept moving on the water. Because the boat drifted at a different speed than the smoke, there was never enough time to get set up in one place the way we wanted. As well, the ocean swells were *so* high, I didn't want to get down too low either. All we needed was a boat mast punched into the bottom of the plane."

One of the fishermen from the ill-fated *Paula and Jordan* waits to be hoisted into a Labrador helicopter hovering overhead. The ferocity of the storm which lasted the vessel is not apparent in this picture, but soon after the photo was taken, the boat was swamped by waves and sank. (Canadian Forces photo by Bill Barber)

After several attempts to hover directly above the boat, and after just as many near misses, Kelly Jamieson succeeded in getting the big yellow helicopter properly lined up. Morawski threw down a line, Barber grabbed it, and with Taylor's help, hooked the oldest Dawe to it, and he and Barber were in the air again. This time they reached safety. Morawski helped Mr. Dawe inside. Barber went back to the boat, got Jimmy Oakley into the horsecollar, and was brought back up with him. The whole procedure — getting the hatch ready for hosting, several attempts to get the chopper into position, and the two hoists themselves — took over two hours. Two hoists to go.

But the helicopter was almost out of fuel.

"We finally got two guys off," Jamieson continues, "but the other two fishermen were still down on the boat, along with Tom Taylor. We knew the other helicopter was coming, but we also knew we *had* to get out of there right away or we would have to come down in the ocean. However, Bill Barber flatly refused to leave without his partner. So the hook was lowered, Tom grabbed it, and Bill and Kevin hauled him inside. Then we headed for Cape Race."

"I was really quite worried because we had to leave the boat," Bill Barber adds. "Because I knew the shape of the boat by then, and what the ocean was doing. Leaving those two guys was a terrible decision, but we had no choice."

"When I saw the helicopter leave, I never thought they would be back," Bill Dawe explains. "I knew what the winds were like, and I didn't think they would ever send another chopper out. Now there was just my brother and me...."

At about this time, Shellie Dawe answered the phone at home. A good friend was on the line, and Shellie recognized concern in the woman's voice — concern about the fate of the *Paula and Jordan* and the men on board.

"My friend knew about the mayday," Shellie said, "but no-one wanted to tell me. She called because she thought I had better know. She had known since morning, but thought it would be best if I wasn't told until the helicopter had taken everyone off. She went on to say that the chopper had come back, but that only two of the men were on it. She didn't know which two.

"I lost it then. I left our two kids with my mother and raced into St. John's. On the way, I stopped at the convenience store where Jeannie worked, and told her there was trouble on the boat, that the boys were in danger, that the boat was sinking, that they had sent out a mayday.

"Jeannie was so calm. She just looked at me and said, 'I know that.'

"'You what?' I asked.

"'I know that,' she said again. 'Mom told me this morning.' Later I got the story of my mother-in-law's premonition. She had been so right. But then I went on into St. John's to a longliner owned by our friends. I knew I could hear the marine radio there. Within an hour, about twenty other members of the family were there as well."

"When we got to Cape Race, the winds were really strong," Bill Barber continues, "but the other chopper came in at almost the same time. Because of the winds, it was never shut down. Tom and I jumped out of ours and climbed into the other one and away we went again. It took us an hour to get back to the boat, but at least things went okay this time. We got the other two guys off safely."

Bill Dawe is hoisted into a Search and Rescue helicopter just before his fishing boat sinks in an Atlantic Ocean storm on June 18, 1992. Three other men were rescued in the same incident. (Canadian Forces photo by Bill Barber)

Then the *Paula and Jordan* rolled over and sank.

"By the time we got back to land, we were all pretty relieved," Barber admits. "We picked up the two fishermen at Cape Race and then flew all four to St. John's. The families met them at the airport, and I went into town to the Health Sciences Centre because I had been banged around a bit. I did not get a chance to meet the rest of the Dawe family until much later.

"In the summer of 1996, CBC Television in Newfoundland did a story about the rescue on their program *Land and Sea.* Because of it, I was able to talk to the Dawes. There hadn't been much time out on the boat."

Shortly after the television program aired, Jimmy Oakley, who now lives in Ontario, was shown a tape of it. He looked at it with the greatest wonderment, and when it ended, admitted that he had no memory whatsoever of the entire rescue. The shock of what had happened was just too strong. He never fished again. Nor, for that matter, did Bill Dawe, Sr.

The day after the rescue however, Bill Dawe was out fishing again — on another boat. Bill Barber and Tom Taylor, meanwhile, were back in the air. A man on a boat had had a cardiac arrest.

And the *Paula and Jordan* was only a memory.

17

By Parachute at Night

Jacques Daigneault loves to hunt, but late in the afternoon of September 27, 1993, he almost died doing so. He was at Lac du Trappeur, a small, isolated body of water four hundred miles north of Montreal. The nearest settlement was a place called Lebel sur Quevillon. With Daigneault were his brother Guy, and two brothers-in-law, Sylvain and Daniel Chagnon. They had all been flown to the hunting camp four days earlier, and had directed the pilot to pick them up at the end of the week. This was the first time the group had hunted in such a remote area.

"I was worried about the fact that he was going so far into the bush," explains Francine, Daigneault's wife, "but I know that hunting is important to him, so I would never try to talk him out of it. I did insist, though, that he take a radio with him. Then, if anything happened to me or the children, we could at least get in touch with him."

Just hours before he departed, Daigneault agreed — though somewhat reluctantly. He rented a High Frequency radio for ten days, and the cost, when split four ways, amounted to only thirty-five dollars per man. It was probably the best thirty-five dollars he ever spent.

During their time at Lac du Trappeur, the hunters slept in a tiny cabin close to the shore. Immediately behind the building were hills, most of which had been logged in previous years. Old stumps were all over the place, as were mounds of earth torn up by the loggers. At one time, the area had also been scarred by forest fires.

Jacques Daigneault's troubles began after a day of moose hunting across the lake from the cabin. He and Guy had shared a small boat on the trip back, while his brothers-in-law rode in another. The Chagnons reached shore first, so by the time Jacques and Guy got back and had their boat secured, Sylvain and Daniel were unloading their weapons and making sure they would be ready for the next day.

Suddenly one of the guns, a 30.06 calibre rifle, went off.

The sound of the shot cracked sharply in the pre-dusk light, echoed from the surrounding hills, and died out somewhere in the hazy distance. The bullet hit the outside of Jacques Daigneault's lower right leg, ripped through flesh and bone, and exited. It then grazed his left leg just forward of the Achilles tendon. The latter wound was minor.

Daigneault fell to the ground, his face a mask of pain, fear, and disbelief. One minute he was healthy, happy, and looking forward to a good meal at the close of a long day. The next, he was writhing on the rocky foreshore with part of his leg missing and his life changed forever. His blood already stained the place where he lay.

The shock of what had just happened was almost impossible to comprehend, but within seconds, Daigneault's companions rushed to his aid. Desperately, they attempted to staunch the flow of blood, which by this time seemed to be everywhere. One of them slipped off his belt, wrapped it around Daigneault's right thigh, tightened and tied it there. The tourniquet was makeshift, perhaps, but it was the only thing available. Someone else ran to the cabin for towels, long underwear, a shirt — anything to stop the haemorrhaging. Guy Daigneault held his brother, talked to him, assured him everything would be okay, and did his best to comfort him.

By the time the men had carried Daigneault into the cabin and placed him on the floor there, somebody remembered the HF radio.

The instrument did not work too well, and there were some delays, but word of the accident finally got out. It would be several hours before help arrived, however.

SAR Techs Dan Lamoureux, left, and Andy Ainslie parachuted in the middle of the night into a lake in northern Quebec to save the life of a critically injured hunter.

In the "SAR Mission Report," an official summary of the response to the accident, the Rescue Co-ordination Centre at Trenton indicates that a Hercules aircraft was tasked to respond at 11:20 P.M. The plane departed Trenton at 12:25 A.M.; on board were Jacques Daigneault's life-savers. A Labrador helicopter took off soon afterwards.

"From what we were told later," said Dan Lamoureux, a SAR Tech on the Herc that night, "the radio the hunters had did not work well enough to reach the authorities up there. I believe somebody had to walk somewhere to get help. That HF radio sure helped later on, though."

Andy Ainslie, the SAR Tech team leader, was fearful about what he and Lamoureux might find. "When I was told that the gun the man had been shot with was a 30.06, I was worried. I knew that type of gun, and I knew the kind of damage it could do. Because the rifle was so powerful, and because the guy had been down for so long, I knew time was pretty important now. In fact, it was critical."

Scott Case, a former Brantford, Ontario high school geography teacher, was the aircraft commander that night. "We knew the place we were heading to was in the middle of nowhere," he recalls, "but at least the weather was good when we set out. We knew it would be marginal later on, and that was not good. If our guys had to jump to this guy, they needed everything in their favour.

"I remember talking to Andy Ainslie on the way up. We had known each other for some time, and we had a good working relationship. We went over the procedures we would follow once we got there. I couldn't believe how calm Andy was. He wasn't nervous in the least, and I know he was glad to be on the mission. The guy's a real pro."

The trip to Lebel sur Quevillon took the Hercules a little over two hours, and by the time they reached the area, the weather was closing in. There was cloud over parts of the bush, and when the aircraft came down low enough to attempt to locate the lake where the injured man was waiting, those on board could see almost nothing — not even a light on the horizon.

"Thank God they had the radio," Dan Lamoureux says, "because without it, we never would have found them. It was never very clear, but we were pretty happy when we heard them — and I know the feeling was mutual. There was a bit of a language barrier, but we were able to let them know what we needed.

"We told them to light a fire somewhere close to where they were, and we would be guided by it. The fire was a pretty small one, but everything in the area was so black, it gave us something to focus on."

The SAR Techs dropped flares, so they could get a better idea of what the terrain was like in general, and in back of the cabin in particular. But after getting a glimpse of how rough the land was, they decided that the jump would have to be into the lake. The Herc made additional passes overhead, and on these Lamoureux and Ainslie tried to determine just where in the lake, what the wind speed and direction were, and what the drift would be once they hopped off the ramp door. By now, the weather front was almost upon them. Already freezing rain had been reported in the higher elevations.

By this time, the Labrador helicopter that had been dispatched from Trenton, with SAR Techs Ron Rae and Arnie Macauley, was getting closer, although it was reporting weather-related delays en route.

"We knew we couldn't wait around any longer," Andy Ainslie explains, "so we called the people on the ground and asked if they could get a boat out on the lake to pick us up if we drifted too far. We would each carry about seventy pounds of stuff on the jump, but we wanted to make sure we kept our medical equipment dry. We knew we would need it for the injured man as soon as we got to him."

Up in the cockpit, Scott Case confirmed the readiness of the SAR Techs, circled over the hinterland bordering the lake, and lined up for the final pass. The jumpers checked each other's equipment one last time, walked to the edge of the open ramp at the back of the plane, then leaped out into the night. Master Corporal Richard Miron, the loadmaster, announced their departure. The Herc continued to circle.

"Andy jumped first," said Dan Lamoureux, "and because we went into cloud almost right away, I couldn't see him, but I knew he was directly below me. For a few seconds I was afraid I might come down onto the top of his parachute canopy. I remember thinking I'd better not keep following him because I wasn't sure how fast he was going; if he was turning, if he was slowing up — whatever. I didn't want to hit him, so I did a left-hand turn because I knew the water was on my left, and I wanted to come down in it rather than going over onto high ground. And even though we were only in cloud for about ten seconds, it seems pretty long when you are under canopy and can't find your partner.

"When we came out of cloud, we were about five hundred feet above water. I landed first, in the water, and Andy was about twenty feet away. Fortunately, we were just in front of the bonfire, but it was pitch-black on the lake itself. The hunter who came out in the boat almost ran over Andy. However, we didn't need to be picked up because we both swam to shore."

Both SAR Techs went right to the cabin. Lamoureux says he sometime thinks back to that night, from the perspective of the hunters: "I've often wondered what they thought, not just of the plane going over and over and the flares, but of these two strange guys in black wetsuits, wearing helmets and carrying bright orange sacks, walking out of a lake in the middle of nowhere."

That night, however, neither SAR Tech had time to do any wondering.

"The victim was lying on the floor when we entered the cabin," Ainslie explains. "The light was not very good, only one lantern, but we did as well as we could. I took his vitals and Dan started to have a look at the leg. The guy's blood pressure was very low, and he was obviously in a lot of pain. The wound itself was quite significant, and ugly. The bullet had entered the right leg, where the calf would have been, and blew that portion away, along with the bone structure. His leg was really only still attached by some skin and maybe one or two ligaments. The foot would rotate almost 180 degrees."

"We knew we had to get some fluids into him right away," continues Lamoureux, "as well as morphine to ease his pain. He was a real fighter, and was more or less conscious, but both tired and groggy after what he had gone through. The morphine helped him relax a bit, because for hours now he had been tense with all the pain. And of course, we knew we had to get him out of there as soon as we could, and we didn't want to see him suffer any more than absolutely necessary. We hooked two IVs into his arms and then, once the morphine started to work, we began to do what we could to stabilize the leg. We got his brother to tell Jacques to bite down on a glove while we moved the leg around so it could be packed and splinted. The brother held Jacques' hand while we did this.

"We checked the left leg as well, but it didn't seem to be bleeding, so we concentrated on the right one. It was always so hard to see properly though, and it was really hot in there. The fire had to be kept going to keep Jacques warm, but because we were in our wetsuits, we were sweating all over the poor guy. We held our flashlights in our mouths, but after a while, the batteries started to go."

While the SAR Techs worked on their patient, the circling Hercules they had just left called down to say that the helicopter was twenty to thirty minutes back, and that if conditions were at all favourable, they would hoist the victim out. Ainslie told Sylvain and Daniel Chagnon to be sure the fire was going so that the Lab pilot, Captain Paul Kruis, could pinpoint the spot.

"After we got Jacques stabilized, his blood pressure started to come up a bit, and his vitals were looking better," Ainslie explains. "He was out of shock and communicating some, but he was also very tired. Our biggest concern had been that he would remain in shock because of all the fluids he had lost. We had actually run out of fluids by that time, and had nothing more to give him. We were glad when the chopper arrived."

Daigneault was placed on a Stokes litter and hoisted into the Lab from about sixty feet. Macauley and Rae eased him through the right door of the helicopter and lowered him gently into the back of the aircraft. Then Dan Lamoureux came up on the hoist and brought Guy Daigneault with him. Ainslie followed with some of the medical gear. As the plane turned to depart, the last flare from the overflying Herc dropped into the lake. It was almost morning.

*   *   *   *   *

Helicopter 308 flew directly to the town of Amos, but by the time of its arrival, the threatening storm had become a reality. Captain Kruis was unable to land, and instead had to shortly thereafter do an IFR (Instrument Flight Rules) approach into Val-d'Or. Jacques Daigneault was taken by ambulance to Amos. He spent a month in treatment there and then was placed under the care of a specialist attached to the Pierre Boucher Hospital in Longueuil. The former mechanic with the City of Montreal was not able to work after his accident, but his spirit never failed him. And even though doctors had to shorten his leg by some three and a half inches, he is determined to regain a normal life. He has been hunting — this time with bow and arrow — and last winter he learned to skate all over again! Someday he hopes to see Dan Lamoureux and Andy Ainslie, and thank them for saving his life.

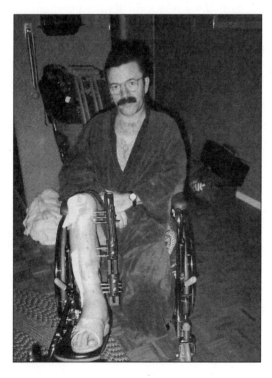

Photograph of Jacques Daigneult taken during his recovery from the gunshot that badly shattered his right leg. He is wearing a metal "Orthofix" which is held by eight bolts drilled into his lower leg. (Photo courtesy Jacques Daigneult)

*   *   *   *   *

As for the two SAR Techs, they were lucky to walk away from SAR Daigneault. When the helicopter flew to Lac du Trappeur the next day for the parachutes and other equipment left behind, the crew was able to get a daylight look at the area where Dan Lamoureux and Andy Ainslie landed. Instead of the rather placid lake surface they expected to find, they saw exactly the opposite. The lake bottom near the bonfire was nothing but snags, deadheads and debris. The SAR Techs had come down, in the darkness, into the one area that would not have left them severely injured or perhaps killed. That area was less than fifty feet across. None of the floating logs and broken tree trunks had been visible from the air the night they jumped.

18

The Cruel Sea

T he television footage of the search is dramatic. On the surface of the heaving sea, the people cling to their raft and wave to the plane overhead. Survival equipment is hauled to the open ramp of the aircraft, then pushed out into the screaming wind. A second later, the staccato radio voice of the loadmaster announces that the drop is complete. The Hercules does a climbing turn and leaves. Whether any of those desperate souls will be able to reach what's been dropped is anybody's guess.

The above scenario took place in a raging North Atlantic storm on the night of December 8, 1994, during a search for survivors from the ship *Salvador Allende*. The air drop was from a plane from Greenwood, Nova Scotia, and Tom Furlotte was a flight engineer on board.

"I have been involved with Search and Rescue for quite a while," he told this author, "but I have never experienced a storm like the one we flew in that night. We were beaten up really badly, and the turbulence was unreal — unbelievable.

"One of my jobs on board the Herc is to sit between, and just behind, the pilot and first officer. During searches, the flight engineer keeps an eye on the airspeed and altitude. While the pilot is flying the plane, he can look around, watch where he is going and so on, and the first officer backs me on the instruments and keeps an eye on the temperature, engine torque and all the other stuff.

"On that search, I could hardly read the air speed indicator. First of all, our lights were dim in the cockpit anyway, but there was so much lightning outside that your eyes would start to adjust to the darkness, and then there would be half a dozen lightning flashes in a row, and you were blinded. But the speed changes of the aircraft in the turbulence were scary. The plane would lurch ahead, then slow down quickly, then speed up. The gauges at times were just a blur. We were all wearing headsets, of course, and using the intercom, but with the engine noise, the heavy, heavy rain outside, and all the thunder, you had to yell to be heard. We were five hundred feet above the ocean.

"Neither the pilots nor I got airsick, but a lot of the rest of the crew did. Our poor navigator, Richard Dumais, who was at his little table at the right rear of the cockpit, was terribly busy all night, and he had a hard time keeping his dinner down. But the guy who really should have received a medal was a cameraman from CBC Television. I've forgotten his name now, but I remember him as a big guy with a beard who really knew his job. He was lugging this huge camera around, on his shoulder, and the thing must have weighed fifty pounds. He would shoot a bit of film, grab his barf bag, shoot some more film, and get sick all over again. I felt sorry for him. He earned his pay. You can see from the television footage that the plane is up and down, and lurching all over the place. Believe me, that cameraman was doing the same thing, as was almost everyone else."

The *Salvador Allende* story began far from the stormy North Atlantic. Owned by the Black Sea Shipping Company out of Odessa, Ukraine, the vessel was just under five hundred feet long, and carried a crew of thirty-one — twenty-nine men and two women. Named after the late Marxist president of Chile, the ship was twenty-one years old. At the time of the storm, it was carrying a load of rice from Freeport, Texas to Helsinki, Finland. It had cleared the harbour at Freeport on December 2. All crew members were Ukrainian.

As far as is known, the trip from the Texas port, around the southern tip of Florida, and up the eastern seaboard of the United States had been uneventful. Though the water in the Gulf Stream was relatively warm, the ship began to encounter worsening weather as it moved northward. The storm that it attempted to ride out was not only vicious out on the ocean, but also created havoc in Newfoundland as well: electricity was out for twelve hours, every shopping centre was closed in St. John's, and heavy snow, blown by high winds, blocked most highways in the eastern part of the province.

At 10:15 P.M. on December 8, the *Salvador Allende* declared a mayday. The storm-battered ship was taking on water, and the skipper believed it was going to sink. He ordered his crew into lifeboats.

Flight engineer Tom Furlotte was one of the last people to see the ship *Salvador Allende* before the vessel sank in a wild Atlantic storm in December, 1994.

"We were called at about 11:00 that night," recalls Tom Furlotte. "I know I had just gone to bed when the phone rang. It took us a few minutes to get to the airport, but we were in the air in an hour. Because we had been told that a ship was sinking and people were already in the water, or about to go in the water, we knew the urgency of the call. But everyone was in in no time, and that included the people from CBC who had been on the base doing a story on SAR Techs. I think they got more than they expected on that trip though. They were not too keen on going out the next day.

"The weather in Greenwood was actually not bad, but as we got out over the ocean, we knew it would be different. About two hundred miles out, we could see lightning in the distance, and the winds were picking up. The last reported position of the ship was 632 nautical miles southeast of Halifax."

On board the Hercules from Greenwood that night were two SAR Techs, Ron O'Reilly and Andre Hotton. The loadmaster was Marco Michaud. Captain Kevin Dort was first officer, and flying the plane was 30-year-old Captain John Forrest. All of them were experienced. Forrest had flown Hercs for six years.

By the time the men from Greenwood got close to where they were headed, they had been informed that at least one other aircraft was going to join them. It was also a Herc, in this case an American plane from Elizabeth City, North Carolina. The subsequent air and sea search necessitated by the *Salvador Allende* was co-ordinated in New York City, at the U.S. Coast Guard Center.

"When we got close to where the ship was supposed to be, we went down to five hundred feet and started to look," Furlotte explains. "And sure enough, it was fairly close to the same place. At first we noticed that the lights were not very bright, but then we realized that they were actually underwater. The ship was listing to port, and the entire bow was underwater. The stern of the ship, where the bridge was, was sticking up out of the water. We called RCC in Halifax, gave them the exact position, and said that yes, the boat was sinking, but that it had not gone down as yet. At first, we couldn't see any people so we circled around and came back over the same place. We did that *one* circle — one circle only — and the ship had disappeared. It sank that fast.

"In the back, Hotton and O'Reilly thought they could see a light on the water. They were wearing night-vision goggles, and we had all the rest of our lights out, and that includes the outside blinker lights, so the night vision equipment would work. Then the SAR Techs confirmed the sighting, and dropped a SKAD. We had no way of knowing whether or not it reached the people in the water."

The SKAD (survival kit — air droppable) is a remarkable recent addition to Search and Rescue equipment. Canadian-designed, it is the result of civil and military co-operation. Almost nine feet long, the sea-SKAD is made up of two liferafts, some medical supplies, a radio, blankets, and especially food. It can be the difference between life and death to someone stranded at sea, and can accommodate twenty people. It is now used in several countries.

"By this time, we heard that there were more than twenty people in the water," Furlotte continues. "A ship captain had radioed that in, and RCC confirmed it for us. There were several ships heading for the area, but we did not see any of them at this time. We just kept on searching as long as we could take it, and after a while, went up higher to get above the storm. At least it was calmer there. The Herc from North Carolina replaced us."

Even though the Canadian plane might have been above the storm for a while, the weather down below was as furious as ever. Ships rushing to the rescue were in peril themselves, though no others suffered the fate of the *Allende*. One that came close was the *Delaware Bay*, a container ship that happened to be in the same general area at the time. Wild winds and waves tore forty-one railcar-size containers off the ship and damaged others on the deck. The vessel later limped into Halifax for repairs.

After about an hour, as soon as John Forrest felt that his crew was somewhat refreshed, he descended back to the five hundred foot level. It was dawn, and the first streaks of the eastern sun illuminated a desolate sea. Bits and pieces of junk seemed to be strewn everywhere, and no-one knew whether it was all from the *Salvador Allende* or not. Now the true nature of the ocean surface was readily apparent. For miles, as far as the eye could see, waves the height of five-storey buildings swamped all before them. Ron O'Reilly recalls the heartbreak involved when survivors were seen; often little could be done for them. "We dropped everything we had," he says, "but in the end, I guess all of it was lost."

Tom Furlotte remembers seeing one of the SKADs hit the water: "It came down on top of a wave, and then shot at least a hundred yards before it even touched down again. We never saw it again.

"We kept circling over that part of the ocean, and noticed pallets, or chunks of things that would float, and one or two people would be holding onto them, but you couldn't tell at times whether they were alive or dead. In one case, we found a liferaft, and we could see people clearly. We dropped a SKAD to them, with a radio, and they got the radio going. We almost cheered when we heard a guy's voice. He said there were eleven on the wooden raft, but that the raft itself was breaking up. Every time wave hit it, they would lose another couple planks. The raft was originally fully covered, but by the time we saw it, the top had been broken away.

"We talked to those people twice, I think it was. The man was hard to hear, and he spoke only a little English. We all listened as closely as we could, and as a group, put together what he said. The navigator took everything down.

"By this time, we were getting really tired. We had been in the air for hours, and our fuel was low. But shortly before we turned for home, we saw one man in a little dory, or what looked like a rowboat. He was just sitting there, and whether he was alive or dead was impossible to tell. Later on, though, two or three days later, other planes saw the guy sitting there. Apparently he had tied himself into the little boat and died in it — sitting up."

Andre Hotton remembers that "there were others we saw who were alive." He describes in anguished terms how difficult it was to see survivors in the water, to see them wave, and to know he had nothing to give them.

To an outsider, what the men on that Hercules saw and experienced that night is almost impossible to comprehend. As far as is known, none of the people they tried to help survived. Yet they gave everything, including their personal survival kits, in an attempt to save lives. Finally, at the end of a terribly stressful and worrisome flight, Forrest and his crew left the search area. Their gas supply was dangerously low. By the time they got home, they had been in the air for eleven hours — almost all of it in severe turbulence.

In all, twenty-nine people perished following the sinking of the *Salvador Allende*. Two men were rescued.

During the afternoon of the day the ship went down, another vessel heading for Norway plucked Iban Skiba, the second officer, out of the water. The 37-year-old was dazed but not otherwise incapacitated. Two days after the sinking, Sergeant Jim Dougerty, a U.S. rescue specialist, jumped from a helicopter to the aid of a stricken survivor. The man, Alexander Taranov, a 36-year-old father of two, had bobbed in a lifejacket for all those hours, unable to see because the ocean brine had damaged his eyes. He was taken on board an American Pavehawk helicopter and flown to Dartmouth General Hospital. Within hours, he was sitting up in bed and talking on the phone to his wife Larysa at home in Odessa. She had not known of the tragedy. Taranov recovered fully.

In the days that followed, the search went on — but those involved knew that hopes of finding more survivors were not good. No doubt many, and perhaps most, drowned. Others probably died from exposure. Some may have been killed trying to get off the ship. Ultimately, the cruel sea claimed her own in various ways. Two days after the sinking, sharks were seen devouring corpses.

Canada's Rescue Co-ordination Centres are often busy places. Here, three men at the Trenton RCC are checking the last known position of a missing plane. They are (L to R): Wayne McRae, Don Gargano, and Kevin Grieve.

Epilogue

As of this writing, there are 120 Search and Rescue Technicians in Canada, while an additional eleven are in training; of those eleven, one is female. Their graduation will bring the complement up to the Preferred Manning Level of 131. It is expected as well that the number of women entering the trade will greatly increase in the future.

SAR Techs respond to air, land and sea disasters anywhere in Canada, excepting in our larger urban areas, where organizations already exist to cope with emergencies. To qualify for the trade, students must be able to deal with problems of every kind by doing many things: parachuting, scuba diving, mountain climbing, and — more than ever before — performing advanced paramedical procedures .

There are three Rescue Co-ordination Centres in Canada — in Halifax, Trenton, and Victoria — but SAR Techs themselves are located in several places across the country. Wherever they may be based, their work is second to none.